A Time for Change

A Time for Change

How White Supremacy Ideology Harms All Americans

Martha R. Bireda

ROWMAN & LITTLEFIELD
Lanham • Boulder • New York • London

Published by Rowman & Littlefield
An imprint of The Rowman & Littlefield Publishing Group, Inc.
4501 Forbes Boulevard, Suite 200, Lanham, Maryland 20706
www.rowman.com

6 Tinworth Street, London SE11 5AL, United Kingdom

British Library Cataloguing in Publication Information Available

Library of Congress Cataloging-in-Publication Data

Names: Bireda, Martha R., author.
Title: A time for change : how white supremacy ideology harms all Americans / Martha R. Bireda.
Description: Lanham : Rowman & Littlefield, [2021] | Includes bibliographical references. | Sum-
    mary: "The starting point for eliminating the virus of white supremacy ideology from our culture
    must be in our educational system. This book is intended as a vaccine to help eliminate the
    damage and to prevent future generations from being infected."—Provided by publisher.
Identifiers: LCCN 2021000812 (print) | LCCN 2021000813 (ebook) | ISBN 9781475857412 (cloth) |
    ISBN 9781475857429 (paperback) | ISBN 9781475857436 (epub)
Subjects: LCSH: Multicultural education—United States. | Anti-racism—Study and teaching—Unit-
    ed States. | Whites—Race identity—Study and teaching—United States. | White supremacy
    movements—United States. | Social justice and education—United States.
Classification: LCC LC1099 .B52 2021 (print) | LCC LC1099 (ebook) | DDC 370.1170973—dc23
LC record available at https://lccn.loc.gov/2021000812
LC ebook record available at https://lccn.loc.gov/2021000813

♾ ™ The paper used in this publication meets the minimum requirements of American
National Standard for Information Sciences Permanence of Paper for Printed Library
Materials, ANSI/NISO Z39.48-1992.

To the first African and European bondservants who lived in harmony fifty years before racism was thrust upon them for the gain of others.

Contents

Foreword

From 1865 to 1898, a little-known miracle took place in my hometown of Wilmington, North Carolina, a pleasant-looking, flower-filled, pine-tree-laden port city. It's the seat of New Hanover County, a peninsula bordered by the Cape Fear River, the Intracoastal Waterway and the Atlantic Ocean. Founded in 1739, Wilmington, located in what is called the Lower Cape Fear region, has always been a very isolated place, out of reach for most of the state. The county is situated on the southeast end of the state and resembles the tip of a woman's high-heeled shoe. So, it was no wonder that the rest of the world didn't know about this fascinating nineteenth-century inspiring miracle.

After the Civil War, Wilmington had become what some newly freed African slaves called a mecca. They had heard and some had read that there were good jobs and opportunities in Wilmington. They started moving there so much so that within a few years, blacks made up the majority of what turned out to be a very prosperous city. They were able in a short time to turn Wilmington into a model for other freedmen to show them how they could attain political, economic, and social status so soon after the war.

By the 1890s, Republicans (black and white) were able to join hands with the newly conceived Populist Party and win elections. In fact, the state's governor and United States senator were both Fusionists. John Hope Franklin has written: "In 1894 such a combination seized control of the North Carolina legislature. Immediately, the Democratic machinery was dismantled and voting was made easier, so that more Negroes could vote. Negro office holding soon became common in the eastern Black Belt of the state. The fusion legislature of 1895 named 300 Negro magistrates. Many counties had Negro deputy sheriffs, Wilmington had fourteen Negro police, and New Bern had both Negro policemen and aldermen. One prominent Negro, James H. Young, was made chief fertilizer inspector and director of the state asylum for the blind; and another, John C. Dancy, was appointed collector of the Port of Wilmington" (Franklin, 1967).

By October 1897, the city of Wilmington (population, 1890 census: 10,089 whites and 13,937 blacks) was completely governed by Fusionists. Mayor Salis P. Wright, a Republican, and his board of four black aldermen (Andrew J. Walker, Owen Fennell, Elijah M. Green, and John G. Norwood) and six white aldermen (W. E. Springer, W. E. Yopp, B. F. Keith, A. J. Hewlett, D. J. Benson, and H. C. Twining) held office. Other

ix

black officeholders included: Charles Norwood, the New Hanover County treasurer; Henry Hall, assistant sheriff; Dan Howard, city jailer; John Taylor, customs bookkeeper, and David Jacobs, county coroner.

Wilmington's white Democrats resented these nine black officeholders. They contended that the city's black population was becoming "insolent" and "impudent." One Democrat wrote: "Conditions in Wilmington were becoming unbearable. It had become most uncomfortable for white women and girls to appear on the streets, as some of them had been elbowed off the sidewalks by colored women. Many colored men were insolent, because political developments had given them an erroneous idea of their position in public affairs. Their white leaders had misguided them while making suit their own selfish ends" (Howell, p. 178).

In January of 1898, the white Democrats prepared "quietly" but "effectively" to overthrow the fusion government. A group called the "Secret Nine" (Hugh MacRae, J. Allen Taylor, Hardy Fennel, W. A. Johnson, L. B. Sasser, William Gilchrist, P. B. Manning, E. S. Lathrop, and Walter L. Parsley) met at the home of Hugh MacRae to map strategy. The city was divided into sections and men were placed in charge of each area. The whites also armed themselves with repeating shotguns, rifles, and pistols. "I doubted if there was a community in the United States that had as many weapons per capita as here in Wilmington," boasted one of the "Nine." The group, however, decided to adopt a wait-and-watch policy. They feared harsh reprisal from the local Fusionist authorities whom they dubbed "The Big Four" (referring to Dr. Salis P. Wright, the mayor; G. Z. French, the former postmaster of Wilmington and acting sheriff of New Hanover County; W. H. Chadbourn, the postmaster; and F. W. Foster). The "Nine" detested the "Four" because they "controlled the majority voters, the Negroes, who always voted the Republican ticket as that was the political faith of their emancipator, Abraham Lincoln. This control of the Negro vote assured these Republican office holders a continuity in the office and local influence" (Hayden, p. 3).

The white Democrats were convinced that they had to recover their government for economic reasons too. They had become frustrated with the number of blacks with higher paying jobs. They agreed that this practice was retarding the city's growth. One local Democrat wrote: "Negroes were given preference in the matter of employment for most of the town's artisans were Negroes, and numerous white families in the city faced bitter want because their providers could get little work as brick masons, carpenters, mechanics; and this economic condition was aggravated considerably by the influx of many Negroes, and Wilmington was really becoming a city of Lost Opportunities for the working class whites" (Hayden, p. 2).

Wilmington also had a substantial black business and professional community. The white Democrats complained of the stiff competition four lawyers (Armond W. Scott, L. A. Henderson, William A. Moore, and

L. P. White) gave their white counterparts. The whites also detested the fact that the city had two African American physicians.

On November 11, 1898, the miracle came to an end when the displaced wealthy white Democrats, after months of propaganda, planning, and agitation, whipped a group of heavily armed middle-class, and poor whites into a frenzy, took over the government and set in motion what would later be incorrectly called "The Wilmington Race Riot of 1898," a bloody event that was actually a massacre and a coup that left countless blacks injured, dead, and many run out of town. The event was significant because it ushered in the white supremacist movement of the twentieth century which is still with us today.

This book is a clarion clear call for the Wilmington, North Carolina, miracle to make a comeback to prove that the only solution to the race problem in America is for middle-class, working-class, poor white and black folks to get together, prosper, work, live in peace and to most of all, not betray democracy. It is also a scholarly, well-researched book that makes plain that the idea of "whiteness" and white supremacy should be and is dead on arrival in the twenty-first century and that it will be null and void for years to come.

Larry Reni Thomas
Chapel Hill, North Carolina
Fall 2020
Author, *The True Story Behind the Wilmington Ten*
Participant in the award-winning documentary
film *Wilmington On Fire*

Acknowledgments

First of all, I owe a huge debt of gratitude to Tom Koerner, who had the courage to say go for it, to have the trust in me to write this book and to wait patiently as it was revised during the coronavirus pandemic. Thank you, Tom.

Many thanks to Carly Wall and other Rowman & Littlefield staff who worked to bring this book to fruition.

Words cannot truly express my gratitude to my dear friend and editor, Colleen Clopton, for her excellent editing skills and for our Sunday afternoons chats about the purpose of being a writer.

Thank you to Randy Jaye, author of *Perseverance: Episodes of Black History from the Rural South*, for his thoughtful and insightful critique of the manuscript. Your comments were invaluable are greatly appreciated.

My sincere gratitude to Larry Reni Thomas for his insightful and thought-provoking foreword. The foreword related to the Wilmington, North Carolina, "miracle" as he refers to it, provides a model for healing racism in America.

In a small town such as where I live, interlibrary loans are the lifeblood of the writer. I could not have done the tremendous amount of research required for this book without the skill and assistance of Claire Myers, the library technician at the Mid-County Regional Library of Charlotte County, Florida.

I thank PeggyDawn and Robert Moran for their commitment to this project. Their "Enlightened Whiteness" conversation was essential to helping readers understand at a personal level, the issues raised in this book.

I wholeheartedly thank Jennifer French, owner of the Yoga Sanctuary in Punta Gorda, Florida, for providing the venue and co-facilitating the Sister-to-Sister: Conversations on Race sessions that addressed the ideas presented in this book. I thank the twenty-one participants whose openness, honesty, and willingness to explore the topic of "whiteness" was inspiring and fueled a feeling of optimism about racial healing in our nation.

Thank you to my friends, Nancy Staub, Maureen Peters, Myrna Charry, and Kim Wilcox your encouragement and support during this writing process.

Finally thank you to my two greatest supporters, my children, Jaha Cummings and Saba Bireda. Jaha thank you for your review of the manuscript and inspiring afterword. Saba, thank you for your continued encouragement and support.

Introduction

In the spring of 2020, two viruses leaped to the forefront of American conscious-ness: first came the coronavirus; it was followed by exposure of the virus of white supremacy ideology that has infected the collective American mind for over three hundred years.

The initial manuscript of this book was completed and submitted to the editor at the end of February. In March, however, everything changed in America, including the publication of this book. On March 13, the American public received the Emergency Declaration concerning the ac-tuality of the COVID-19 virus in our midst. The pandemic grew, and racial incidents involving the murder of African Americans were brought to light, the most explosive being the murder by a policeman of George Floyd in Minneapolis. Floyd's murder was the catalyst for protests across the nation and the world.

Floyd's murder, like nothing else, pulled the cover off American ra-cism and revealed the fallacy and consequences of white supremacy ideology that has held both blacks and whites hostage for more than three hundred years. This book, changed and shaped by the events of the spring of 2020, reflects the need for readers to become aware of, acknowl-edge, confront, and challenge the damage done by white supremacy ideology to all Americans, regardless of the color of their skin. Now, the ideology of white supremacy and the culture it has created in this nation must be examined.

White supremacy is the idea that white people are inherently superior to those of other races, especially the black race, and those designated and perceived as "white" have the right to dominate them. It is a very powerful ideology that promotes whiteness as the ideal for humanity and the epitome of the social hierarchy. The historically social construct of "whiteness," the focus of this book, is a creation of white supremacy ideology. The ideology uses race to create differences and to legitimize social, economic, and political exclusion. It provides for the collective and individual privilege or advantage of those designated and perceived as "white."

American society is deeply separated and unequal based upon skin color. The beliefs, values, and ways of interacting are infused with the idea of white superiority. It is important not only to associate white su-premacy ideology with extreme and explicit hate groups and racial ter-rorism. The idea permeates and is perpetuated in all American social, political, and economic institutions—education, law enforcement, health care, and so on—in that every institution establishes unfair policies and practices based on race that create discriminatory treatment and the impacts of such treatment.

White supremacy ideology undergirds American culture. Culture is defined as a learned set of shared perceptions about beliefs, values, and norms which affect the behavior of a relatively large group of people (Lustig and Koester, 1996). American culture is founded on a set of beliefs, values, and norms that support the ideology of white superiority. In American culture, the belief in separation rather than the connection and interdependence of humankind is reinforced and perpetuated.

Separation is the basis of white supremacy culture, primarily racial separation; however, in a subtle and masked way, social class is intimately connected to the idea as well. Ultimately, white supremacy is a historical system of exploitation, domination, and oppression created to maintain the wealth, privilege, and power of the ruling elite. It is the premise of this book that white supremacy culture is damaging to all Americans, white as well as people of color.

To understand how American culture became based on the ideology of white supremacy, we must look at its very beginnings as a colony. What we all learned as history in school was incomplete, embellished with images of settlers enjoying a new life in a new country free of the restraints they had left behind in Europe. The beginning chapters of this book provide a different picture, one that makes cognizant the history of white servitude in America. This history, one of holding whites in bondage, has been hidden to create and reinforce the fallacy of white supremacy.

In the chapters that follow, the reader will learn the how and why of "whiteness": the social construction created from white supremacy ideology; the methods by which Americans were indoctrinated by white supremacy ideology; how it has shaped American culture; its consequences; how the white supremacy ideology has kept those designated and perceived as "white" blind to their manipulation; and finally, how white Americans can become free of the virus of white supremacy ideology. This book is intended as a vaccine to help eliminate the damage and to prevent future generations from being infected.

Chapter 1: Before "Whiteness"

In this chapter, the "invention of the mythical America" is examined. The chapter includes the history of European enslavement in colonies, which preceded African slavery, and which has been oddly omitted by most historians. The chapter also describes the bondage conditions of Africans as indentured servants; all Africans did not arrive as slaves to the colony of Virginia. The accomplishments of Africans who were released from their bonds are discussed as well as the harmonious relationships and intermarriage between European and African bondsmen.

Chapter 2: The Invention of "Whiteness"

The brutal treatment of European and African bond servants is explored along with their resentment which caused many of them to run away. This chapter examines the impact of the multi-racial Bacon's Rebellion and its threat to the powerful elite in Virginia. Because of the fears this rebellion raised, "whiteness" was quickly and deliberately designed as a method of divide and conquer.

Chapter 3: The White Supremacy Culture

The social construction of "whiteness" based upon the premise of "separation" imbues every aspect of American culture. In this chapter, the beliefs, values, and norms of white supremacy culture are discussed. Most critically, the symbols of black inferiority and the ways in which they were and are utilized to reinforce and perpetuate white supremacy ideology within American culture are examined.

Chapter 4: The Indoctrination of White Supremacy

In probably the most critical chapter, the process by which the collective American mind for generations has been implanted with white supremacy ideology will be examined. The major sources by which white supremacy ideology was/is reinforced and perpetuated in American culture will be discussed.

Chapter 5: The Impact of "Whiteness" Indoctrination

The four states of whiteness, that is, blind, perverse, toxic, and enlightened, are discussed as well as specific responses exhibited in each of these states. Attachment to the social construct of "whiteness" can produce psychological impairments; distorted reality, the lack of empathy, and racially conditioned emotional needs being the most critical.

Chapter 6: The Promise and Limits of "Whiteness"

The privilege of whiteness has not and is not experienced in the same way by all persons who identify as white. In this chapter, the marginalization of yeoman and poor whites, as well as the psychological benefits of "whiteness" will be discussed. The racialized culture created by white supremacy ideology, and the classism that keeps many working and poor whites at the margins will be examined.

Chapter 7: The Time for Change

The COVID-19 pandemic exposed both the racism and classism pervasive in American society. The ideology of white supremacy and the assumptions based upon that belief must be acknowledged, confronted, challenged, and changed. Guidelines for change—acknowledgment, recognition, and willingness—are presented.

We cannot return to who we were as a nation before COVID-19. The murders of Ahmaud Arbery, Breonna Taylor, and George Floyd, and the resulting nationwide protests have made America look at its racist past and present. As a society, we must do better, be better. This book is written as a patriotic endeavor to help all Americans recover from the "virus" of white supremacy ideology that has separated us from each other and the ideals that would make America a great nation. We must marshal the resources, passion, fervor, conviction, and will to eliminate the virus of white supremacy ideology that exists in our culture, just as we battle COVID-19.

Because the collective American mind has been infected with the virus of white supremacy ideology, we as individuals must engage the critical work of reflection to uncover, acknowledge, confront, and challenge the indoctrination that has been thrust upon us. "A Primer for Enlightened Whiteness" offers to opportunity to begin this process.

This book is especially intended to be used by educators, trainers, and so forth who provide instruction of any sort in our schools, colleges, law enforcement agencies, and all other institutions.

It is in our schools, in particular, that the ideology of white supremacy has been nurtured, reinforced, and perpetuated. The starting point for eliminating the virus of white supremacy ideology from our culture must be in our educational system. It is imperative that authentic and true American history be taught, that policies and practices which reinforce white supremacy ideology be eliminated. We must not let another generation of American children be infected with this virus.

ONE

Before "Whiteness"

Was there a time in this land known as America when those designated and perceived as white and black lived and worked together in harmony? Was there a time when the color of one's skin did not determine one's status in life? Yes, before the virus of white supremacy ideology came to these shores, America was different. Europeans and Africans related, connected, and allied on the basis of their common humanity and life conditions.

1619

When the first Africans reached the shores of the Virginia colony, there were no "white" people there. The settlers were designated as either English, Christian, or their nationality. When the Africans arrived, the population consisted primarily of three groups of people; the landholding aristocrats, a small yeoman class, and a large peasant class consisting of involuntarily indentured European servants and slaves. In August 1619, "20 and odd Negroes" arrived in the Virginia colony; this is considered the beginning of African slavery in the Virginia colony.

The first "white" settlers had no concept of themselves as "white" men, according to historian Lerone Bennett Jr. The legal documents of the period identified those who would become white as Englishmen and Christians. Early documents identified the nationality of all non-Englishmen as Irish, Scotch. Africans were identified as Negro, from the Latin word "niger" meaning black in both Spanish and Portuguese languages. The first Africans who arrived in the colony of Virginia had been stolen from Portuguese slave traders by British pirates. This is the group of Africans referred to as the "20 and odd Negroes."

This chapter explores four aspects of actual colonial history that had to be distorted or omitted by the ruling elite to create a new history, an alternative to the truth of the early days of the American colonies:

- the class-based enslavement of Europeans,
- the indentured versus the enslavement status of early Africans,
- the achievements and class status of free Africans, and
- the harmonious multiracial relationships and class alliance among the indentured class.

SEVENTEENTH-CENTURY BRITAIN

Three social classes existed in seventeenth-century Britain:

- Peasant: the lowest class, agricultural workers who were bound to the landlord's domains and not allowed to own land, to move or migrate; not allowed to own weapons, vote, serve on juries, or testify in court against an aristocrat; not allowed to grow their own food or make their own clothing; and would be punished by death for raising a hand against a landlord, even in self-defense.
- Yeoman class: the freeborn yeoman owned a plot of ground, was subject to the landlord's rule but had traditional rights; in return yeoman were required to carry weapons and most importantly be ready to form rank and crush any peasant uprising that might threaten the landlord.
- Upper class was comprised of the aristocracy, the landlords who had power of life or death over his peasants. A peasant had no rights a landlord had to respect. A landlord could work peasants to death or sell them. Landlord aristocrats lived on the backs of peasants and were protected against servile insurrection by their large yeoman buffer class.

Multitudes of English citizens were desperately poor in Britain during the early seventeenth century. The roots of the problem lie in the transfer of common land during the twelfth and thirteenth centuries. During that period, landlords began to enforce property rights by instigating enclosure, meaning that land which had been farmed in common was now fenced off, and peasants were evicted from the land, causing widespread poverty and starvation.

The result of these bad policies was that the colonies were considered critical to the stabilization of England as the nation experienced growing crises in poverty, homelessness, and lawlessness. Fearing that Britain would soon be overwhelmed by the poor and the lawless, the crown designated the colonies as the "dumping grounds" for English convicts, poor and homeless children and women, many of whom were prostitutes; with questionable backgrounds the rootless, the unemployed, the criminal, and the dissident. Those exported from Britain to the Virginia colony, deemed as "surplus people" and dumped there as slaves, were British convicts, poor English children, and the Irish. These individuals were kidnapped with official approval, forced into the galleys of boats, and sold to planters when they arrived in Virginia.

Their lives belonged solely to the planters; they had no rights, thus they were more slaves than servants. Primary sources provide evidence of the status of the first slaves to arrive on American soil: they were European, not African. The tenor of their experience, however, set the tone for the future enslavement of Africans.

INDENTURED SERVITUDE

Poverty and hardship drove emigrants from England, Scotland, Germany, Switzerland, and Ireland to the British colonies. Many of these came as indentured servants who agreed to work for a period of three to seven years without wages to pay for the cost of their passage to America. For many, the voyage did not conclude in dreams of prosperity and freedom but in poverty, the articles of indenture binding them in slavery.

Our conventional understanding of an indentured servant is one who voluntarily agrees to place himself or herself in bondage to another human being for a specific number of years. The images that have been placed in the collective American mind is of indentured servants' hopeful travelers making the voyage from Europe to the colonies to escape religious or other persecution and to start a new prosperous life in Virginia. The fact is most came involuntarily.

Some eighty thousand persons were deported from Europe during the colonial period. According to Hoffman (1991), "All those unfortunate people were to become slaves with white skin, indentured servants who were indeed slaves in every sense of the word until they gained their freedom. Nor did all gain that freedom when their terms of servitude expired. By 1636, of the 5,000 persons in Virginia, 3,000 had come to the colony as servants."

BRITISH CONVICTS

By the time of the American Revolution, England had transported upward of seventy thousand convicts to her New World colonies — Virginia, Maryland, Barbados. Their crimes? Vagrancy, petty crimes, behaving like dissolute youth. A 1615 ruling gave King James the legal authority to rid England of what were labeled poor, lawless woman and children by shipping them away to the New World. This was not emigration but forced migration.

POOR CHILDREN

Poor children who had no homes, who slept in public places and lived by begging and thieving were a nuisance in London during the sixteenth and seventeenth centuries. These vagrant children were perceived by the elite as the next problem of which to be rid.

In 1618, the authorities in London began to sweep up street children from the London slums, ignoring the screams and weeping of parents. The first 100 children arrived in America around Easter of 1619, four months before the arrival of the Africans. By 1627, some 1,500 kidnapped children had been sent to Virginia. Other shipments of children followed; most of these children would die before they reached adulthood.

THE IRISH

A third group of forced emigrants to the American colonies were the Irish. Irish and Anglo-Irish landowners, dispossessed of their land by the British for one infraction or another, and political prisoners became a continuous shipment to the colonies during the reigns of James I and Charles I.

The Irish were regarded as inferior people; the English had misrepresented them through negative imaging. Because of the success of this stereotyping, there was no outrage when the Irish were "displaced" to the colonies. Their disappearance was justified.

In 1625, James I of England proclaimed that all Irish political prisoners be transported and "sold as slaves" to English planters in the American British colonies and British West Indies. He saw this transport of Irish slaves to the colonies as the solution to the problems of the "unwanted and surplus" people in Ireland and the shortage of labor in the colonies.

Historian Herbert Byrd notes in his book, *Proclamation 1625: America's Enslavement of the Irish*, that: "Upon arrival in the colonies, the Irish slaves were put up for sale by the ship captain or merchants who owned them. Families who made the passage together to the New World were often separated and each sold to the highest bidder. They were paraded before the bidders like cattle at a livestock auction. Their teeth were sometimes checked, and many had to strip naked for the buyer's inspection."

The British did not discriminate according to class when they stole and sold Irish nationals. Bookkeepers, scribes, and teachers as well as the illiterate were equally made slaves. Because all Irish were regarded as an inferior race compared to the English, any group of people considered as barbaric, backward, savage, lazy, and apelike as the Irish were deemed made good slaves. The treatment of them in the colonies was extreme. Whippings were meted out with little thought because, in addition to their other barbarities, they were Catholic, troublemakers all.

Interestingly, while the African and Irish slaves were housed together, the Africans were better fed and beaten less often. Several reasons account for this. First, Africans were more expensive to acquire; second, they were selected because of their skill in the cultivation of tobacco and because they were naturally acclimated to the weather in Virginia; and third, the beastly stereotypes attributed to the Irish were not yet assigned to them.

The twenty or so Africans who arrived in August of 1619 were not immediately considered to be enslaved and were given the same designation of indentured servant as the Europeans before them. Official records indicate that no laws were passed during this time declaring Africans to be enslaved. In court records of the Virginia Company, the citation of authorities indicates that the first generation of Africans fell into the same socioeconomic category as the first forced European immigrants. Although Africans were integrated into an involuntary labor system that had nothing to do with skin color, they were still treated better.

After their terms of indenture, Africans as free men had the same rights and privileges as other free men. Africans were able to accumulate land, vote, testify in court, and mingle with Europeans with equality. Free Africans became artisans, shopkeepers, lawyers, physicians, and skilled farmers.

The headright system developed by the Virginia Company of London encouraged the importation of bond laborers and indentured servants. The system offered a legal grant of usually fifty acres to settlers who paid the transportation costs for the importation of workers who would become indentured servants. Sweet (2000) posits that as a result, some Africans were able to use the importation of African and European workers as a route to a higher social status, some becoming aristocrats.

Anthony Johnson—once an indentured servant—and his family are a perfect example of indentured Africans who won their freedom, purchased land, bought indentured servants through the headright system, and became part of the landowning class in the colony. Primary records indicate that Anthony Johnson, Richard Johnson, John Johnson, and Benjamin Dale owned tidewater plantations and left large estates. According to Byrd (2016), these Africans were established members of the ruling class.

In 1666, about three hundred of Virginia's colonists were of African ancestry. At that time 11 percent of African colonists and 18 percent of Europeans colonists owned either land or slaves. The social status of Africans during the first forty-seven years after their initial arrival on the shores of Virginia is indicative of a class-based rather than race-based society.

Englishmen and Africans interacted with each other on terms of relative equality for two generations according to Breen (2004), African settlers were part of the social structure of the colonies. African and European men and women socialized and married based on social class. Inter-marriage was common, and the possibility of a genuine multiracial society became a reality during the year before Bacon's Rebellion in 1676.

CONCLUSION

The American colonies were established by aristocratic elites, not the English yeoman class. Upper class beliefs and attitudes toward the lower classes were transferred to the New World. Aristocrats and gentry who established the colony of Virginia believed in and practiced separation by class. It is somewhat unrealistic to believe that aristocratic and masterful men from Britain, imbued with a class consciousness, would be able to create a new nation which promised liberty, freedom, and equal opportunity for all regardless of class.

The feudal system and peasant labor were all that these men knew; they had no consciousness or experience in creating a free and equal society where masters and workers would be of the same class and share the benefits of labor. Indentured labor was absolutely critical in creating and maintaining agricultural wealth in colonial America as it was in the United Kingdom itself. The rules of English peasantry were implanted in America as a system of servitude and slavery.

Virginia, the first English colony, was a class-based society. The colonists who regarded themselves as Christian or English were respected and awarded based on their class position—not their skin color. For purely economic reasons, whiteness and racism were introduced more than fifty years after Africans arrived in Virginia. This decision, created for the purpose of greed and for maintaining the power of the ruling class, changed the social structure of the colony from a class-based to a race-based society.

Had historians provided an accurate account of the beginnings and social structure of the early Virginia colony, and if students from grade school to college were honestly educated on the beginnings of whiteness, perhaps the mythology of white supremacy would not have taken hold in the collective white mind, and America might have become an honest beacon of freedom.

TWO

The Invention of "Whiteness"

What brought the virus to the people who came to the shores of America? What made the organism vulnerable to the virus?

"The race problem in America was a deliberate invention of men who systematically separated blacks and whites in order to make money."
—Lerone Bennett Jr., *The Shaping of Black America*, 1975

Before you begin to read the passage below, close your eyes and consider the image that comes before you when you say "American" to yourself. More than likely, you will see the image of a person designated as "white" in this society. The America that we and the world knows is a white nation.

Before 1680, however, as stated in chapter 1, America was simply a nation of peoples of different nationalities, there were no people identified as "white" here. There was a lack of racial animosity and hatred. They lived harmoniously in a "class-based" society.

Tobacco plantations became money-making entities for the aristocratic gentry of England who had both the political capital and financial resources to invest in the Virginia Company. The Virginia Company, also called the London Company, was an organization of merchants and wealthy men in England, chartered by King James I. As an agricultural venture, the company's intention was to make vast amounts of money while exploiting the labor of bond servants and slaves. The backbreaking, non-ending work required a pliable, obedient, captive workforce.

Two factors were the chief catalysts for the class of wealthy planters with political connections to create a race-based rather than class-based society in Virginia. One strictly for economic reasons, and the other related to the fear of rebellion among the servile class. First, African labor was thought to be more profitable than continuing to import Europeans. While the initial purchase price of Africans was more expensive, they were thought to be a better long-term investment than Europeans who would be held in bondage for a limited number of years. The Africans selected for enslavement had agricultural skills, especially with tobacco cultivation.

Second, the ruling class feared that rebellion among the bondmen might be imminent for a number of reasons. The idyllic life of indentured servants portrayed in America history books was far from the reality of bonded servants. Life as an indentured servant was hard, brutal, and at times even violent.

Many similarities exist between the experiences of European indentured servants/slaves and African slaves. According to Dulles (1966), like Africans, European men, women, and children were kidnapped or spirited away by unscrupulous agents. These unfortunate immigrants made the trip across the Atlantic under the same horrendous conditions as Africans later suffered on the Middle Passage. As with Africans, the immigrants were forced into the crowded holds of ships, enduring unsanitary conditions, hunger, and thirst. Sickness and disease engulfed them and at least 50 percent died before they reached the Virginia shores.

Once these European immigrants reached the new continent, they were sold by ship captains or agents to planters. As with Africans, families were broken up and workers sold to the highest bidders. European slavery was the precedent for and foretold all the brutality that Africans would later endure.

The conditions under which indentured servants labored, like those imposed on Africans during racialized enslavement, are detailed below:

- backbreaking, sunbaked work in the dirt sunup to sundown;
- half-day and Sunday off if all work completed;
- a meager diet—a biscuit at noon, greens for dinner when they got back to the quarters after dark;
- rigidly confined to the place of indenture; no freedom of mobility;
- excessive punishment, such as extension of terms for minor offenses;
- the violence and brutality of whippings, branding, and other corporal punishment by master for disobedience or laziness;
- the brutal rape of females;
- prohibition from voting or engaging in trade;
- inability to marry without the consent of master;
- penalty an extra year of servitude if rule disobeyed; and
- absolute obedience and submission to master required.

As great a factor for discontent among the European bondsmen along with their brutal treatment was the frustration and sense of betrayal experienced by tenants and men who had completed their terms of servitude. Believing in the rhetoric of freedom and prosperity for all who came to the American colonies, these now free men looked forward to working for themselves and making a good future in tobacco. However, as more bondservants became free, they posed a potential problem for the ruling class by their planting tobacco and increasing the volume of the product which then depressed prices.

In response to this threat, the ruling class created a number of restrictive conditions, according to Battalora (2013):

- imposing as long a servitude as possible before allowing the servant to become free;
- increasing the length of servitude as a penalty for running away, giving birth to a child, or killing a hog;
- adding penalties such as reimbursement for presumed losses to master when absent, or for loss of crop, in order to double the time of service;
- servants who did become free after 1660 found it increasingly difficult to locate workable land that was not already claimed, which forced them into tenancy, or move out into the frontier on Indian land; and
- in 1670, a law was enacted that directly impacted these "free" men. They were stripped of their ability to vote so that only landowners and keepers of houses could vote in elections.

The actions taken against the freed Europeans tenants and servants fueled their frustration, anger, and resentment toward the ruling class. In addition, bondservants European, African, and Native were all angered by the treatment they received from masters. In 1661, indentured servants rose up in rebellion over inadequate food. There were at least ten other popular revolts or insurrections that brought together Europeans and Africans before the spectacular revolt of 1676.

BACON'S REBELLION

Before the Rebellion, tensions were high in the colony because over the years dissatisfaction with the ruling class had grown. Bondservants European, African, and Native were all angered by the treatment they received from masters. Interracial groups of runaways had become a major problem for the planter class. In the same year as Bacon's Rebellion, between eight hundred to nine hundred European, African, and biracial slaves fled Virginia in large groups to form tri-racial groups with Native Americans; they were called Maroons.

The elite wanted to keep the servants and the poor as uneducated, disenfranchised and as ignorant as possible, but now grievances had finally reached a boiling point. In 1676, an alliance of European, African, and Indian bondservants, as well as freed servants and small landowners, united in a fight against the ruling elite who governed the colony.

RULING CLASS FEAR

The alliance between the frontier's men, freemen, and servants, both African and European, presented the greatest threat and danger to the ruling class. The ruling elite saw the possibility of "class consciousness" and became aware of their vulnerability. The threat of a united labor force to the plantation system was clear and would not be tolerated.

According to Morgan (1975), in addition, the ruling class faced a huge problem that no other colony had ever faced. Of the 15,000 adult colonists, 9,000 were slaves and 7,000 of the 9,000 were visibly of European descent. As was the model in England, a yeoman buffer class had to be created to prevent a revolt. This yeoman class had to be approximate in numbers to its enslaved European population. The solution was that European slaves had to be transformed into yeoman.

CHOICE OF TOOL OF SOCIAL CONTROL

Allen (1997) stated that "It was in the period after Bacon's Rebellion the 'white race' was invented as a ruling-class social control formation." The new white buffer class, with no real change in class status in the colonial social hierarchy, was given an illusionary status based upon skin color. Now as whites, they were set apart from the African bond laborers, and they suddenly had the authority to rule over and oppress Africans. At the same time, however, as common whites they would be subjected to an unending economic inequality. Established on the basis of skin color, this divide and control strategy created a caste system—one of European descent and the other of Africans—and three social classes, the elite landholders, the yeomen, and the slaves including split biracial families.

THE "WHITENESS" CONDITIONING PROCESS

European indentured servants and freedmen had to be recreated as white people. They had to learn the meaning of whiteness; the limited privilege they were going to be given. The ruling elite had to make the Europeans believe that because of skin color they were more important than before and had the same interests as elite whites because their white skin made them superior to Africans. In order for the concept of "being white" to mean something, it had to make a difference in the lives of the newly white; "whiteness" had to have what could be perceived as some tangible value.

Segregation and white privilege were used to entice Europeans into becoming white.

Living quarters and meals once shared by Africans and Europeans were now segregated. Europeans received better clothing. This deferential treatment served the psychological purpose of making whites believe they were superior to their black counterparts. While the newly white operated under the illusion of superiority, the reality of their lives did not change in a material or economic sense. The Irish in particular received the same brutal treatment as before becoming white.

The imposition of whiteness kept the minds of common whites focused on their new sense of superiority and privilege. What they did not perceive was the way in which they were being used as pawns by the planter elite. Rather than a consciousness of their common reality as an oppressed class, the same as blacks, they aligned themselves with the interests of the ruling class.

THE IMPOSITION OF LAWS

To set in stone the divide-and-control mission, the ruling elite set about passing a set of laws that impinged upon the freedom of both blacks and whites, especially white women. These laws took away the basic human right to choose whom one desired to love and to marry. Males in the slaveholding class were still capable of having exploitative and illicit sexual relationships with enslaved women, while designating the child of such unions as holding the same social status as the mother, common white men as well as blacks and Native Americans were legally denied to right to choose whom they could love and marry.

The very first laws designed to destroy and deny normal human connections were anti-miscegenation laws (the outlawing of interbreeding between different races) which were enacted during the colonial period. Until these laws were forced upon the population, persons of European, African descent, and Native peoples lived, worked, socialized together, loved, and married each other. In 1691, Virginia was the first colony to pass a law forbidding whites and free blacks to marry, followed by Maryland in 1692.

Because miscegenation had been openly practiced, there was a large biracial population that presented a problem of passing. The ethnicity of the mother of a child born in the colony was critical; the child would be born free or enslaved depending upon the status of the mother. A 1662 act protected ruling-class Englishmen who fathered children by enslaved women and ensured an increase in the enslaved population; however, a child born of a free white woman and a black man was of critical concern to maintaining the slavery system. All children born in the colony would be bond or free according to the condition of the mother.

- 1662. Act XII. Children got by an Englishman upon a Negro woman shall be bond or free according to the condition of the mother, and if any Christian shall commit fornication with a Negro man or woman, he shall pay double the fines of the former act.

- 1696. Act I. This act mentions the same difficulties and names special penalties for the fornication and adultery of servants and repeats the historic passage, be it enacted that all children born in the country be bond or free according to the condition of the mother. (Guild, 2012)

A 1691 Virginia law, Act XVI was directed toward whites, but particularly to "white female slaves." The law stated:

- 1691. Act XVI. And for prevention of that abominable mixture and spurious issue which hereafter may increase as well by Negroes, mulattoes, and Indians intermarrying with English, or other white women, it is enacted that for the time to come, that whatsoever English or other white man or woman, bond or free, shall intermarry with a Negro, mulatto, or Indian man or woman, bond or free, he shall within three months be banished from this dominion forever.
- And it is further enacted, that if any English woman being free shall have a bastard child by a Negro she shall pay fifteen pounds to the church wardens, and in default of such payment, she shall be taken into possession by the church wardens and disposed of for five years and the amount she brings shall be paid one-third to the majesties for the support of the government, one-third to the parish where the offense is committed and the other third to the informer. The child shall be bound out by the church wardens until he is thirty years of age. In case the English woman that shall have a bastard is a servant, she shall be sold by the church wardens (after her time is expired) for five years and the child serve as aforesaid.
- 1696. Act I. This act mentions the same difficulties and names special penalties for the fornication and adultery of servants and repeats the historic passage; be it enacted that all children born in the country be bond or free according to the condition of the mother. (Guild, 2012)

Some Virginia State Statues were deliberately designed to restrict the freedom of whites with regard to the choice of mate:

- 1792. Chapter 42. "For preventing white men and white women intermarrying with Negroes or mulattoes, it is enacted that whatsoever white man or woman, being free, shall intermarry with a Negro man or woman, bond or free, he or she shall be committed to prison for six months, and pay $30.00 for the use of the parish."
- The initial punishment was to ban the couple from the colony. Many interracial couples fled to Maryland or Pennsylvania. In 1696, performing an interracial marriage became a criminal offense for ministers, who would be fined 10,000 pounds or tobacco or defrocked if he had no assets. The new law also required ministers to

preach against interracial marriage from the pulpit or to be de-frocked.

- In 1715, a law directed against white women in particular was im-posed. "Women were given seven years of slavery and their mixed-race child was automatically given 31 years of enslavement." (Guild, 2012)

CHANGES IN THE STATUS OF FREE BLACKS IN VIRGINIA

The freedoms, privileges, and lives of free blacks would change drastical-ly in Virginia. The world that they knew and experienced was uprooted by the creation of "whiteness." One of the first acts of the ruling class was to take away the African settlers' right to own European slaves. Ultimate-ly, they were segregated, some enslaved, others forced to leave the colo-ny. It was the passage of laws rooted in white supremacy that altered their status in the colony. The laws cited in Black Laws of Virginia: A Summary of the Legislative Acts of Virginia Concerning Negroes from Earliest Times to the Present pertaining to free blacks are found in the Appendix C.

CONCLUSION

Before the creation of whiteness by the ruling class, racial animosity ap-peared not to exist; rather, both Europeans and Africans worked, lived, married, raised families, and lived in harmony. The British view of the poor, plus greed, created the need for free labor and a means to control the masses of European free and bond servants. The fear of the elite was ultimately alleviated through the invention of "white" people. Bacon's Rebellion provided the impetus to create a race-based society. The idea of whiteness and racial superiority implanted into the minds and hearts of common Europeans took root. Whiteness offered individuals oppressed and treated brutally because of their class status an opportunity to iden-tify with the ruling class.

Ultimately, the imposition of "whiteness" served the purposes of the ruling elite when created during the colonial era and the legacy continues to impact American society. Racism as a tool of social control has pre-vented:

- the awareness of class consciousness; and
- the unification and alliance of exploited workers, both white and black.

For over three hundred years the creation of whiteness has sustained and maintained both a belief in the mythology of white supremacy and the plutocratic ideology pertaining to the laboring class. While race and racism are predominating issues in the nation today, the strategic use of white advantage aligned with lower class position still makes classism the critical but unacknowledged method of social control in American society.

THREE

The White Supremacy Culture

Once a virus attacks the cells of the organism, it explodes exponentially until the entire organism is infected. Thus, white supremacy ideology came to define and organize American culture.

> "America is inherently a white country, in character, in structure, in culture."
>
> —Andrew Hacker

The culture of the United States was founded, developed, and undergirded by white supremacy ideology. The beliefs, values, norms, symbols, laws, and institutions around which the culture is organized are infused with white supremacy ideology.

Beliefs are learned and interpreted ideas that people assume to be true. Core beliefs influence one's thoughts, feelings about oneself, others and actions toward others. McKay and Fanning (1991) describe core beliefs as influencing our lives by establishing rules for survival, psychological edits by which we cope, as well as setting the tone for inner dialogue by which we interpret events and experiences. Core beliefs guide how we make assumptions. In this chapter, the rules of whiteness, as well as the inner monologue that operates most often at an unconscious, programmed level will be explored.

The core beliefs of humans influence 95 percent of the decisions we make and the actions we take. Our core beliefs:

- are the basic concepts we live by;
- define our identity;
- determine our feelings about ourselves and our expectations for our lives;
- set the emotional tone of our lives;
- determine our feelings of worth;

- establish our basic fears; and
- operate at an unconscious level.

WHITE SUPERIORITY/BLACK INFERIORITY AS CORE BELIEFS

The core belief that undergirds American culture is that those identified and perceived to be "white" are superior to people of other races. "Whiteness" is a social construction, decided upon and created by people with an agenda. It served and continues to serve an economic and political function.

To establish the superiority of whiteness, a comparison or counterbalancing core belief had to be created, reinforced, and perpetuated. Adding "blackness is inferior" was necessary to give verifiable substance to "whiteness is superior." There is no biological or scientific proof of the superiority of whiteness, but without the negative blackness, or a comparison to blackness, there is much less value to whiteness. Whiteness has value because of the dehumanization of blackness. These two ideas—white superiority and black inferiority—were repeated in every possible instance until they became believed as facts and then grew into solid convictions.

Related to the core idea of white superiority and black inferiority are the beliefs that the white "place" or position in the American hierarchy is at the top, and the black "place" or position is at the bottom. These core beliefs operate to perpetuate and maintain a social, political, and institutional culture dominated by those designated as white in the society. This means that advantages at a collective and individual level only belong to whites.

Core beliefs are supported and reinforced by a set of rules and internal monologues. The core belief of white superiority, of white supremacy and the related discussions and interior monologues might sound like the following:

Core Belief: I am superior because blacks (and other non-whites) are inferior. Allied Belief: I am entitled to and I deserve more advantage because I am white. Allied Belief: I must protect my advantage at all costs.

VALUES

Cultural values define what a group considers to be normal or right. American cultural values like core beliefs are infused and shaped by white supremacy ideology. The human condition is one of connection, and interdependence. Individualism, the capstone of American values, focuses on the individual, independence, and autonomy. This value promotes the idea of the individual as the master and control of his or her own destiny. The value of individualism emphasizes the traits of self-reliance, competitiveness, and success measured by the accumulation of property, wealth, status, and power. The value of individualism negates ethnic affiliation and interdependence as well as denying the real human condition.

White supremacy ideology promotes control and domination as an American cultural value. This value includes domination of nature—the environment—as well as the control and oppression of those deemed inferior to whites in the society. Ideals are expressed values that need not be experienced or demonstrated in reality. An ideal expressed as an American value is that of equality of opportunity. While the Declaration of Independence states that all people are created equal, and equality is a stated cultural ideal, this ideal in itself violates the premise of white supremacy. White supremacy ideology holds that those designated as white are superior and worthy of advantage in American culture.

NORMS

Norms are the shared perceptions characteristic of a culture that provide guidelines and rules for appropriate behavior. Norms include the laws or formal and legal mechanisms that regulate the behavior of the group. It is within this context that white supremacy is promoted and perpetuated. From early anti-miscegenation laws, slave codes to Black codes to Jim Crow laws, the American legal system is made up of laws that affirm white supremacy.

Anti-miscegenation laws were enacted in 1691 in the Virginia colony to prevent sexual interaction and marriage between blacks and whites. Anti-miscegenation laws were designed to serve an economic purpose. With the problems related to free bond indentured Europeans, and the appeal of importing and enslaving a larger African population, children from biracial unions posed a problem. White supremacy ideology required pure white blood as opposed to mongrelizing.

In 1857, in *Dred Scott v. Sandford*, the Supreme Court, the highest court in the land, ruled that black people "are not included, and were not intended to be included under the word *citizens* in the Constitution, and can therefore claim none of the rights and privileges which that instrument provides for and secures to citizens of the United States."

Again in 1896, in *Plessy v. Ferguson*, the Supreme Court reinforced Jim Crow laws (the norm of segregation) by upholding the constitutionality of racial segregation laws or public facilities. This "separate but equal" doctrine legitimized state laws reestablishing racial segregation passed after the end of the Reconstruction Era (1865–1877).

Another less discussed yet very potent norm infused in American culture is conformity. The ideology of white superiority requires whites to conform to the mythology. Whites who do not conform to the rule or follow the construct that blacks are inferior can be ostracized, left off the dinner invitation list, and in the worst cases face violence or death as a result of non-compliance. Those committed to the ideology of white superiority must follow the rules:

- Protect your whiteness; do whatever is necessary to protect your white identity and privileges that are yours by Divine Right.
- Monologue: In all situations:
    - Remember: you are white and white is superior.
    - Remember: blacks are the other, inferior.
    - Remember: because blacks are inferior, they are to remain in their "place," a subservient position of second-class citizenship.

Symbols of White Supremacy Culture: Images and Language

Cultural symbols can take the form of visual images and words. White supremacy ideology indoctrination and infusion into American culture was/is achieved through the use of symbols; symbols in the form of visual images and words that convey the ideas and beliefs of white supremacy. The words or labels associated with the images of blacks reinforced the idea of black inferiority.

Recognizing the social and political goals of specific stereotypical images is crucial to understanding their value in a given society. Stereotypical images are created to impact the beliefs, opinions, attitudes, and behaviors of the group targeted to be influenced or indoctrinated.

Stereotypical images are transient in that they are modified depending upon the particular group to be influenced.

The same stereotypes used to oppress and enslave the Irish were used to create racialized slavery in America. Just as stereotypical images and language was used to dehumanize the Irish as uncivilized, an inferior race, barbarous, violent, and lazy, the British systematically began maligning the character of the African settlers. They would be viewed as savages just like the Irish. (Appendix D provides the similar stereotypical images of the Irish later attributed to Africans.)

The divide-and-control strategy involving the separation and strategic privileging of European bondservants was only the first part of the plan to establish a buffer class. The most ambitious plan of social control involved propaganda: an indoctrination program making up a belief in the superiority of whiteness and the inferiority of blackness. The colonial authorities had to dehumanize the African in the minds of the European bondservants. White supremacy ideology was and is infused in American culture through the use of stereotypical images and creates linkages between black skin and inferiority.

THE CREATION OF STEREOTYPICAL BLACK IMAGES

Dehumanizing and distorted images were the basis for establishing the inferiority of blackness as a core belief in the American mind. Images reinforced by racist language are even more powerful tools to elicit specific emotional reactions. Stereotypical images of Africans and African Americans have flourished in the collective American white mind for over three hundred years. These culturally conditioned beliefs define American culture and are enshrined in the nation's cultural institutions; that is, education, religion, health care, criminal justice, and employment. Stereotypical black images perpetuate the beliefs that undergird white supremacy ideology, promote racial separation, and most critically prevent the development of a multiracial class consciousness.

Three categories of African "racial inferiority" were created: intellectual, cultural, and moral. Each image was created to elicit specific beliefs, thoughts, feelings, and actions related to blacks as a group. The primary belief to be held was the inferiority of blacks. Three types of feelings were elicited: security, repulsion, and fear. Each image consciously or subconsciously can trigger or prompt a thought and feeling related to "blackness." A collection of images and accompanying language were created to serve the purpose of perpetuating white supremacy ideology.

Dehumanizing images of Africans and African Americans have been created through every period of American history, from the early colonial era to today to oppress blacks and condition the minds of whites. Old images of the Africans and African Americans have been revised and embellished at key points throughout American history to twist social and political opinion.

The goal of employing dehumanized images of Africans has been very effective in introducing and then reinforcing an ideology of white superiority and black physical, intellectual, cultural, and moral inferiority. This inferiority ideology rationalized the racial enslavement of Africans and African Americans and created a place or position in American society as that of "natural" servants. To maintain a subjugated labor source after the Civil War, the former Confederate states used insidious images for physical, emotional, and social control of the Negro.

THE ENSLAVEMENT ERA

Sambo and Mammy were images created to defend and rationalize the enslavement of Africans and African Americans. Both images reinforced the superiority of white, and Sambo was principally utilized to present a benign portrait of slavery. Sambo had two principal parts to his nature: he was childish and comical. Above all, Sambo was amenable to enslavement, happy despite his condition, grateful for the paternalism of his

master. Sambo was a natural slave-servant. He was nonviolent and hum-
ble. He most often played the role of buffoon, displaying outlandish ges-
tures and physical gyrations.

The Sambo image was designed to portray the African American male
as docile, irresponsible, unmanly, servile, grinning, happy-go-lucky, dependent, slow-witted, humorous, childlike, spiritual-singing, and of
course, watermelon-eating and chicken-stealing. Referred to as childlike,
dependent, happy, and contented, the poor primitive savage was fortu-
nate to have been saved by enslavement. Sambo was an image that provided a measure of psychological safety and security for whites.

While revolts by the enslaved—that is, Nat Turner—influenced the
creation of the image of the violent murdering African, slavery apologists
still wanted to portray the African as a benign, childlike creature, unable
to care for himself. Without enslavement, this primitive creature would
cease to exist, and it was the white man's burden to care for and civilize
him to the extent that he could learn.

Two of the principal stereotypes created for female African Americans
during enslavement were Mammy and Jezebel. The feminine equivalent
of Sambo was that of Mammy, the loyal, faithful maternal figure. She was
the ideal enslaved woman—obese, dark, grinning, and desexualized. She,
like Sambo, also created feelings of safety and security. Mammy is the
fixture of the 1936 novel *Gone with the Wind.* An antithesis of the Mammy
had to be created as well.

Jezebel was the image of the seductive, beguiling, hypersexual, and
lewd African woman with loose morals. It was the oversexualized enslaved woman who was blamed, especially by the mistress of the plantation, for luring the master to bed and producing mulatto children. The
Jezebel stereotype was used during slavery to rationalize sexual relations
between white men and enslaved black women. The Jezebel image rationalized the rape of enslaved black women; the implication being that
white men did not have to rape black women. During the Jim Crow era,
the Jezebel stereotype of the black woman naked or scantily dressed was
portrayed in American consumer culture on ashtrays, postcards, fishing
lures, drinking glasses, and sheet music.

EMANCIPATION/RECONSTRUCTION

The ideology of "place" in regard to whites and blacks in the American
social hierarchy became critical when blacks were no longer enslaved and
the ruling class had to find some way to continue enforcement of black
subjugation. Two images of the black male were created; one to elicit
repulsion and the other fear. The lazy, shiftless, good-for-nothing black
male was brought into focus. Images were created of him shooting craps
on the ground, stealing chickens, and suffering from a hangover. To

counter the idea of black men being capable of holding public office or having freedom of movement, the image of the "dandy" was created. The dandy, portrayed as a gaudily dressed black male putting on airs, ridiculed black legislators.

These images created feelings of anger, repugnancy, and disgust among whites and the need to fully restore white supremacy. The images and the associated language and labels helped to establish Black Codes which restricted the freedom of newly freed blacks and compelled them to work for low wages. Any African American males elected to public office after emancipation were portrayed as ignorant, corrupt legislators who stole government money and pushed whites off sidewalks.

With Emancipation and Reconstruction came the necessity for a new, more threatening image of the African American male. The most destructive and perverse image created of the black man was that of the "Brute." The Brute image and accompanying language was that of an animal-like ferocious beast that reinforced the myth of the savage African. The black Brute was a sexual predator who lusted for and chased after white women. The crime most associated with the black Brute was the rape of white women.

The most enduring emotion elicited during this period as a result of anti-black imaging was fear. Fear was the tool embedded in the white mind: fear of the violent, savage rapist of white women, fear of loss of higher position for men in the class-based southern society. This image of the Brute created a need to control the African American male and was the catalyst for violence in the form of lynching.

THE JIM CROW ERA

The term "Jim Crow" originated from a minstrel show character developed during the mid-nineteenth century. In 1828, Thomas Dartmouth "Daddy" Rice appeared on stage as "Jim Crow," an exaggerated, highly stereotypical, black, awkward, and simpleton character. The Jim Crow era was devoted to the passage of laws, use of language and images that promoted and perpetuated white supremacy ideology. Stereotypes created during the Jim Crow era (1877–1960s) remain deeply embedded in white American consciousness.

The Jim Crow era did more to create anti-black beliefs and feelings than slavery. Laws have been changed—the Civil Rights Act of 1964 and the Voting Rights Act of 1965; however, distorted images of African Americans created during the 1800s remain deeply rooted in the collective American consciousness. Of the countless crimes against African Americans during the Jim Crow era, this is the most destructive legacy.

The Jim Crow racial caste system served as a social control mechanism in two critical ways: laws and customs kept blacks at the bottom of the social hierarchy, and these laws prevented any racial interaction that could possibly lead to social relationships and alliances. Segregation served the interests of the ruling class.

To further dehumanize blacks and to elicit a negative response, images of blacks created during this period were distorted. The mouth, eyes, and extremities were exaggerated. Their mouths were usually opened with and filled with large and carnivorous-looking extra-white teeth, their eyes white and bulging. Their hands were hairy and ape-like. In many depictions, black images were more animal-like than human.

Historian David Pilgrim (2015) says that the Jim Crow system was undergirded by the following erroneous beliefs:

- Whites were superior to blacks in intelligence, morality, and civilized behavior.
- Treating blacks as equals would encourage interracial sexual unions.
- Sexual relations between blacks and whites would produce a mongrel race which would destroy the destiny of the United States.
- If necessary, violence must be used to keep blacks at the bottom of the racial hierarchy.

THE LATE NINETEENTH AND EARLY TWENTIETH CENTURIES

The image of the threatening Brute from the Dark Continent was revitalized. Acts of racial violence were justified and encouraged through the emphasis on this stereotype of the Savage. The premiere of the silent film *Birth of a Nation* in 1915 marked the change in emphasis from the happy Sambo and the pretentious, inept Jim Crow stereotypes to that of the Savage. In this D. W. Griffith film, the Ku Klux Klan tames the terrifying, savage African American by lynching him.

The decades between 1900 and 1930 were the most difficult periods since slavery for African Americans. The white supremacy ideology prevailed. The virulent and anti-black propaganda created racialized anxiety and fear about the loss of place and privilege among whites. With the rise of the Ku Klux Klan, racial violence proliferated. African American communities were destroyed—East St. Louis, Missouri (1917); Ocoee, Florida (1920); and Tulsa, Oklahoma (1921)—and residents were murdered. Through lynching and the destruction of African American communities, the urgent message to whites was that we must put blacks in their place or else.

CIVIL RIGHTS ERA

Blacks protesting for civil and equal rights brought anxiety, fear, and anger to the collective white mind. The belief in "white place" and "black place" in the social hierarchy had to be reinforced. The black image portrayed was that of being anti-white, aggressive, even Communists. Racist propaganda encouraged white terrorism against blacks during the era.

POST–CIVIL RIGHTS ERA

Racist demagoguery took a different turn in the post–civil rights era, one directed as usual toward the white majority but with the usual implications for blacks. It was in the post–civil rights era that denigration of the poor really took root in the collective American mind. The post–civil rights era ushered in different images and language pertaining to the inferiority of blacks, however with different images and language to avoid the label of overt racism. But once again, during the aftermath of the civil rights movement, the two key stereotypes, the lazy black and the dangerous black, were used to influence the mindset of whites.

Gilens (1999) argued that the racialization of poverty images in the 1960s reflected preexisting stereotypes of blacks as lazy, and as such the American public now associated poverty and welfare with blacks, even though there were more poor whites on welfare than blacks. Media coverage from the early 1960s tended to use images and language related to poor blacks to illustrate stories of waste, inefficiency, and abuse of welfare; at the time images of poor whites were neutral.

The indoctrination related to poverty throughout the 1970s and into the recession of the 1980s focused primarily on the perceived problems of welfare and welfare reform associated with blacks. The racial beliefs, attitudes, and assumptions related to poverty generated by this form of coded indoctrination impacted American views toward the poor and played a central role in generating opposition to welfare spending among white Americans.

Since the civil rights movement—into the 1980s, 1990s, and the present—the evolution of "modern" racism, spread by a willing or ill-informed media, has been the most potent purveyor of negative stereotypical black images.

PERSISTENT AND PERVASIVE STEREOTYPICAL IMAGES

The "moral inferiority" of African Americans is the most propagated image in the current American mind. The image of the black Brute is firmly entrenched in the collective white mind in American society. The image and language have evolved to portray the black man as violent, a drug dealer, a criminal. The predator Brute image has in recent years been transferred to young black males walking down the street, several of whom have died innocently at the hands of the police. This culturally conditioned fear of the black male is demonstrated in emotional expression of a Michael Brown appearing "beastlike" or the killing of Tamir Rice, a black boy playing with a toy gun. It is this image that possibly plays in the minds of policemen who kill innocent black men.

The word *welfare*, used in a general way, became coded language for the lazy, licentious "Welfare Queen" whose only ambition in life is to have babies out of wedlock and secure government assistance, paid for by hardworking white taxpayers. In addition, the language of entitlement promotes fear of the underserving blacks and other non-whites unfairly benefitting from social programs, again paid for by whites.

CONCLUSION

The stereotypical images of blacks are an essential aspect of American culture. These images have evolved into culturally conditioned beliefs about blacks in American society. Beliefs about the superiority of whites and inferiority of blacks have been embedded in the collective American mind.

These beliefs infiltrate every American cultural and social institution. Educational access and opportunity for black children are hampered by the belief in black intellectual inferiority; equality in medical care is denied based on an assumption from the enslavement period that blacks endure pain and suffering better than whites; employment opportunities are curtailed and denied because of the stereotypical belief in black laziness and irresponsibility. It is in the criminal justice system in the United States that the impact of white supremacy ideology is most evident. African Americans are more likely than white Americans to be arrested, once arrested are more likely to be convicted, and once convicted more likely to experience lengthy prison sentences.

FOUR

The Indoctrination of
White Supremacy

The COVID-19 virus is transmitted through direct contact, indirect contact (through contaminated objects or surfaces), or close contact with infected people via mouth or nose secretions. The virus of white supremacy ideology was and continues to be spread through an indoctrination process utilizing racial propaganda. White supremacy ideology evolved to infect the collective American mind.

"From the beginning, Europeans had to be re-made into white people. They had to embrace a social description with a core belief system of rules and privileges. Europeans had to be indoctrinated into whiteness," asserts Byrd (2016). In other words, "white" people had to be created from ethnic Europeans. Indentured servants and freedmen had to learn the meaning of whiteness, and how when they adopted the social designation of whiteness, they would have value in the new society.

The masters had already begun the conditioning process through segregation and strategic privileges of European bondservants, but ongoing indoctrination was necessary to fully create the new "white being."

To fulfill the needs of the ruling class, the belief systems of white superiority and black inferiority had to be drilled into the minds of "whites." This went on for generations—a collective American mind based on the ideology of white supremacy was being created. The indoctrination process had to be continuous and intensified whenever the hierarchies of power were challenged or threatened. The stereotypical images used to create the belief system of white supremacy were continuously reconstructed and revised to fit changing economic, political, and social conditions.

The indoctrination process began with a propaganda campaign employing all institutions—churches in particular—to implant ideas of white superiority and black inferiority into the collective American mind. Simultaneously, laws were created to reinforce the propaganda by explicitly denying blacks most rights—voting, access to equal education, or authority of any kind. Most critically, stereotypical images aligned with negative use of language were created to reinforce the core beliefs of white superiority and black inferiority.

THE SOURCES OF WHITE SUPREMACY INDOCTRINATION

White supremacy indoctrination was perpetuated through six major sources in American society: religion, history, social science, popular culture, the media, and most crucially education.

Religion was a popular and effective basis for theorizing on the origins of racial inequality and Negro inferiority. The Bible has long been used to justify the enslavement of Africans. According to I. A. Newby (1965), the central theme of religious racism is the idea that racial inequality is the will of God. The story of Ham, one of the three sons of Noah, was used as a means of justifying the enslavement of Africans within this theology. Africans were said to be descendants of Ham and therefore objects of the curse placed on Ham by Noah. The story of the curse placed was most frequently used to justify the moral inferiority and the servile position the Negro was destined to hold.

From the beginning of the twentieth century, an array of scientific and pseudo-scientific evidence to support the inferiority of the Negro was dumped into the collective American mind. The physical, intellectual, and emotional qualities of the Negro were studied to prove his inferiority. Science and the field of eugenics preached the genetic inferiority of black people. Theories indicating his inferiority related to the size of the African brain, the thickness of the African neck.

Newby (1965) states that scientific racism was used to strengthen popular prejudice by clothing it in a mantle of academic and scholarly authority, and that while studies began with ethnology and anthropology, beginning at about 1900, eugenics and genetics constitute the most important authority on scientific racism.

In addition to these exaggerated and anatomical differences, African Americans were made out to be less sensitive to both physical and emotional pain than whites. For example, black women were thought to experience little pain with childbirth, and to be able to easily bear the loss of a child to death or sale. These stereotypes of the animal-like savage were used to rationalize the harsh treatment of slaves during the era of slavery as well as the murder, torture, and oppression of African Americans following emancipation.

Propaganda that the layman could understand was needed because scientific racism had been conducted by American intellectuals, using terminology beyond the comprehension of common whites. Pseudo historians and novelists presented a simpler version of the inferiority of African Americans to the general white public. In addition, what was taught in US history books by distortion and omission of facts reinforced the mythology of black. If presented at all, African American history was seen as beginning with enslavement in the New World, and ignoring the historical significance of Africa to world civilization.

The popular culture, including everything from literature to postcards and toys, created inferior images of the black, and these images were shared as part of American culture until the civil rights movement of the 1960s. It was, however, through the popular culture of literature, cartoons, postcards, and ethnic notions such as toys, banks, and cookie jars that the caste position of blacks was cemented in the American mind.

It was advertising that had the greatest impact on making the southern image of blacks into the national image, one that remains in the white American mind. Images of blacks in servile and submissive roles as a part of southern culture became subconscious reality in American whites in general. The mammy image, for example, was used to sell breakfast foods, detergents, and many other household items. The most successful commercial expression was "Aunt Jemima" and her maple syrup; Mammy's counterpart was Rastus, the Cream of Wheat cook. By the late nineteenth century, the stereotypical images of African Americans were known and accepted.

The psychic well-being of whites has been cultivated in America by showing them stereotypical images of blacks in inferior positions and situations. These images became popular advertising "hooks" for consumer goods aimed primarily at the white working class. These advertising ploys and objects of material culture served the class and race interests of the elite by allowing purchasers to ignore their own perhaps lower-class background or condition within the white race while identifying with the interests of upper-class whites.

THE ROLE OF HISTORICAL/POLITICAL FIGURES

From "learned authorities" in science and social science to political figures from *Thomas Jefferson's Notes* to the political messages in national campaigns—all these have weighed heavily on providing "factual evidence" to support the inferiority of blackness. From the coded messages regarding "the welfare queen" in the news to the need for law and order (for blacks mostly, if you take note of incarceration rates), re-fashioned stereotypical images, language, and laws have cemented the inferiority of blacks in the nation.

THE MEDIA

In each historical era, colonial to modern times, it has been the media in all of its forms, from anti-black pamphlets, to racist diatribes in newspapers, to the nightly news, that have been the most critical force in reinforcing and perpetuating stereotypical images and language with regard to blacks and other people of color.

African Americans have been disproportionately represented in news coverage in stories about poverty and criminality. Stories about poverty reinforce the stereotype of the lazy, irresponsible black and hypersexual black woman. The most enduring and pervasive representation has been of the black man as the violent criminal. This criminal image harks back to the "Brute" stereotype created after Emancipation, and supports the initial mythology of the moral inferiority of blacks. Even young black males have been stereotyped as "criminal predators."

These images were designed to associate blackness with danger and violence, indoctrinate whites to be distrustful, suspicious, and fearful of black people, males in particular. The ultimate result of this indoctrination related to the criminalization of black males in American culture is racial profiling, mass incarceration, police brutality, and the killing of unarmed black males.

From negative images of black poor during the 1980s, to images of young black "criminals" in the twenty-first century, the media has stoked the fires of racism primarily through fearmongering. The media has had and continues to have the greatest influence on indoctrinating the collective white mind in America. The media in particular has shaped the current fears of non-white domination and loss of white privilege and power.

THE EDUCATIONAL SETTING

It is in the educational system that the ideology of white supremacy has been reinforced and perpetuated. From textbooks to educational policies and practices, the belief in white superiority and black inferiority prevails. Textbooks present a mythological view of American history and its heroes. Slavery in particular is promoted as a benign system of contented Africans whose enslavement was a natural and beneficial role that brought them from a primitive to civilized status. Blackness is most often equated with enslavement. Glaring omissions and distortions persist regarding the resistance of the enslaved to their status, the creditable deeds of African Americans, their contributions including fighting in America's wars, including the segregated military forces of World War I and II. Beliefs in white supremacy are ingrained through the teaching of American history.

Black students and other students of color experience some of the same issues related to white supremacy as do their parents in the larger society. The belief in black inferiority is demonstrated by low expectations for the abilities of students of color and racially disparate discipline practice. Both white and students of color are through the educational process conditioned to inculcate the culture of white supremacy.

THE CULTURAL CONDITIONING PROCESS

DuRocher (2011) describes the indoctrination of white children beginning in childhood. They are taught to fear, disdain, and dehumanize blacks. This process is reinforced through the educational system, popular culture, racist rituals, and racial violence. The ideology of white supremacy has been cultivated in much of the collective mind of America.

We are born tabula rasa, "clean slate." We receive messages from our parents, grandparents, aunts, and uncles—all the people we love and respect—about who we are, the value of our identity, and that of others. When they tell us that a certain group of people is different from us, not as good as us, not to be trusted, or to be avoided, we know no better than to believe them; these are people we trust, people who take care of us and meet our needs.

We receive significant messages through the social learning context— watching, copying, listening, being praised and chastised—and everything does not have to be stated verbally. Non–African American children are taught to fear blacks when they are told to check the security of their car doors when they see a group of African American males walking on the street. Anyone who grew up with the Aunt Jemima or Uncle Mose salt-and-pepper shakers learned a lesson, never stated verbally, about the role of African Americans. We may not know what that role is, but it's something different, because we've never seen salt and pepper shakers that look like white people.

By the same token, as we grow up and are told to respect and honor certain people because they are heroes or leaders or merely adults, we automatically accept the messages they impart to us by the look, by the voice, by whatever means whenever we're paying attention to them. Their messages become another piece of the puzzle that then fits what we believe. When Thomas Jefferson, the quintessential American hero, wrote of the inferiority of blacks, his message became central to the belief system regarding the treatment of blacks in this society.

Beliefs become imprinted at a very early age, by age five or earlier, even if they are based on myths or stereotypes; by age ten are imprinted in our consciousness. Unless the cycle is broken, these stereotypical beliefs are constantly reinforced and passed verbally and nonverbally from one generation to the next. Through no fault of our own, we inherit a false belief system based upon stereotypical images. Ultimately, these stereotypical beliefs which operate at an unconscious programmed level will generate an automatic response.

Autobiographical sources described by Rutledge Dennis (1981) tell us the effects of racial socialization on white children. The most compelling autobiography is that of author Lillian Smith who described the "lies about skin color and culture." These "lies" fall into three categories—fear, mythology of superiority/inferiority/ ignorance:

- lies calculated to sow fear;
- lies intended to be the building blocks in the construction of a self-sustaining racial mythology that is a constant reminder to whites of their superiority and to blacks of their inferiority;
- lies that deepen ignorance about blacks in America; and
- lies that merely create a subterranean understanding that blacks are not as important because the history books barely talk about them and their lives.

Dennis also says that, "It is virtually impossible for the young white child to escape the pressures to conform to racial etiquette. It is known and lived that in no other sector of American life has the pressure to conform been greater than it has been in matters of race. In matters of race, America has been a closed society."

Unless corrected, generations of students develop beliefs from textbooks and history lessons based upon purposeful untruths, myths, and stereotypes. If we are to break the cycle of distrust, fear, ignorance, and violence that white supremacy culture creates, our educational institutions beginning at the earliest grades must aggressively confront and challenge white supremacy ideology if we are to create a future civil American society.

Denise Winn, in *The Manipulated Mind: Brainwashing, Conditioning, and Indoctrination* (2000), says that: "Indoctrinating a culture involves saturating a particular belief system or set of views into people's minds without allowing question or evaluation. Indoctrination goes on and on, constantly reinforcing what psychologists call perceptual set; the tendency to take in information that confirms our existing beliefs or ideas." She states further, "If these assumptions can gain the status of facts when a whole group of people or a nation acts upon them, these assumptions will probably gain the status of facts." This has become the case of black and other people of color in America.

White supremacy ideology is dependent upon racial and social attitudes crafted through the process of indoctrination, involving the social construction of whiteness and the practice of racism. Winn (2000) states that attitude has three component parts: affect, cognition, and behavior. The affective part refers to the emotional response to a person, thing, or concept; the cognitive component comprises the beliefs or knowledge about a person, place, or thing; and the behavioral component covers the way the individual acts toward the person, place, or thing.

CONCLUSION

It is in fact toward whites to whom the racial propaganda is directed, to produce attitudes that support white supremacy ideology. Racial indoctrination produces an affective or emotional response. Depending upon the individual's belief system, obedience to the rules of whiteness, a pathological response may be exhibited toward the black individual or group. Changing racist attitudes by whites toward blacks and other people of color is central to eradicating white supremacy culture in American society.

The indoctrination of whiteness, white superiority, and white supremacy have been so effective that despite the lack of real economic gains and injuries of class suffered by common whites, no major class-consciousness movement has surfaced among them. Blacks, however, have continued to fight their oppression from colonial times until the present day.

Blacks have been forced into a subservient condition in American society through laws, customs, and violence. However, because blacks were not directly indoctrinated by the white elites through language and images, not all blacks internalized the myth of black inferiority as fully as working-class and poor whites who believed in the myth of white superiority. Individuals such as Alain Locke, A. Philip Randolph, Langston Hughes, and Zora Neale Hurston of the Harlem Renaissance of the 1920s and Dr. Martin Luther King Jr. and Rosa Parks of the civil rights movement of the 1960s are proof that all blacks were not conditioned to the idea of black inferiority.

FIVE

The Impact of "Whiteness" Indoctrination

The virus exponentially changes the organism's cells. The severity of sickness experienced by the organism depends upon the degree of infection. Likewise, the extent to which an individual is infected with the virus of white supremacy ideology determines the state of one's consciousness.

> "By using racism, consciously or unconsciously, to divert public discontent and to boost the shaky egos of white groups on or near the bottom, men of power in America have played a key role in making racism a permanent structure of our society."
> —Lerone Bennett Jr., "The White Problem in America," 1970

The core beliefs of white superiority and black inferiority have been embedded in the collective American mind since their introduction during the colonial period, on and on down through generations. Because of their tenacity and emotional appeal, stereotypes of African Americans have endured and been reinforced in individuals and in families as well as in major societal institutions.

The images of moral inferiority and the construction of the African American criminal are the most powerful, persistent, and pervasive of all stereotypes.

Over time, these stereotypical images became part of the cultural fabric of us and our society. They are central to the thinking and behavior of the mainstream society toward the targeted group. Most significantly, the incorrect beliefs that result from these images are generally accepted as truth, they are not questioned, and they remain as part of the core belief structure of the larger society unless changed at an institutional level by good leadership or privately, person to person. These beliefs are endemic in our society; decree or mandate will not change them. By and large, anyone who grows up in the society is influenced by these beliefs.

A stereotype as described by Boskin (1970) is a standardized mental picture representing an oversimplified opinion or an unexamined judgment that is tenacious in its hold over rational thinking. It can be further described as:

- pervasive once implanted in the popular lore;
- an integral part of the pattern of culture which operates within and at most levels of society;
- affecting thoughts and actions at both conscious and unconscious levels;
- operating at reactive levels of thought and behavior; and
- receiving power from repetition.

The purpose of people making up stereotypical images of Africans and African Americans has always been to create racist beliefs and attitudes in white Americans. Indoctrination was directed toward the white mind to reinforce the myth of white supremacy. It was in this juxtaposition with blackness — THE comparison — that whiteness had value.

Stereotypical images were invented to influence the minds of working-class and poor whites so that a white class consciousness would not take hold. Racism, as a practice and tool of white supremacy has been utilized masterfully to prevent economically oppressed classes of working and poor whites from aligning with blacks and other non-whites for collective bargaining and in opposition to the power structure.

The social construction of "whiteness" is just as powerful and appealing to middle-class, working-class, and poor whites in the present day as it was during the colonial, antebellum, and Jim Crow era. Whiteness promises the American dream: freedom, safety, security, the achievement of the American dream through individual hard work and dedication. To be white is to have advantages and possibilities that are not to be shared by blacks and other people of color in the United States. Whiteness offers many benefits, but there is also baggage that comes with whiteness.

Rutledge Dennis in his essay, "Socialization and Racism: The White Experience," asserts that "racism, the tool employed to separate the races, to prevent class consciousness and to preserve the power of the ruling class has done great damage to the dominant white majority as well as the black minority. Whiteness has had the most destructive impact on poor whites, whose delusionary sense of superiority prevents them from forming alliances with others of the same marginalized class."

According to behavioral psychologist Bobby Wright, "Behavioral scientists generally agree that the outstanding characteristics of the psychopathic personality are the almost complete absence of ethical or moral development and an almost total disregard for appropriate patterns of behavior." Several factors in particular associated with whiteness are characteristic of a psychopathic disorder: the lack of empathy, lack of guilt or remorse for one's action, lack of feelings of right or wrong or responsibilities for one's action. All result in an impaired conscience.

The overall effects of attachment to the socially constructed and manipulated identity of whiteness reveal psychopathic attributes and related psychological impairments depending upon the state of whiteness to which one's identity and self-worth are attached. The empathy deficit, distorted reality, and "racially-conditioned emotional needs" are three of the most critical.

Empathy, the ability to understand and experience the feelings of others, is a key virtue of the human condition. The most destructive psychological pathology related to white supremacy ideology is the empathy deficit. The human capacity for connection, interdependence, empathy, and compassion are destroyed by the social construction of whiteness. Empathy is an impossibility, as the value of whiteness depends upon the dehumanization of the black or non-white "other." White supremacy ideology allows one so indoctrinated to act outside of all human moral codes, to engage in acts ranging from discrimination to violence.

In general, whiteness produces a false sense of reality in those attached to the white social identity. Whiteness provides a delusional or false validation. It encourages a mythical sense of a superior self, not based on biological factors or science, but merely a social construction. A validation based solely on the dehumanization of the other, the black. This distorted reality produces delusional thinking or a fixed/false belief about the self and a set of "racially conditioned emotional needs."

Racially conditioned emotional needs relate to feelings generated the mythology of white superiority "place" in the racial hierarchy of the United States and create an irrational need for the mythology of black inferiority. These needs tend to justify and to inflame a sense of entitlement in those attached to whiteness. Racially conditioned emotional needs must be satisfied in some individuals to maintain a cohesive sense of the white self.

Feelings produced by class oppression increase the need to satisfy racially conditioned needs. When one is shamed or "put down" because of low social status, or feeling frustration because of not experiencing the entitlement promised by whiteness, the intensity of racially conditioned needs increases. As the emotional intensity increases, the individual must react.

Feelings related to the "right to have more, and be more" caused punishment to blacks who did not get off of the sidewalk, when approached by a white. Blacks perceived to getting out of their place or being uppity or the sight of something material possessed by a black that a white did not have triggered taking, destroying, or brutalizing the black.

Whiteness and the racism associated with it can produce several effects or states of whiteness: blind, perverse, and toxic whiteness. The individual who is firmly attached to the white identity and derives worth from whiteness will blindly accept this designation without any questioning. The individual who manipulates the institutional power of law enforcement to feel a sense of white power operates in a state of perverse whiteness, while those most anxious and fearful of losing their "place" in the American hierarchy demonstrate and experience a resentment and rage that develops into a "toxic" whiteness which leads to racially motivated terrorism and violence.

Some individuals, however, designated as white, even from childhood question the absoluteness of white superiority and black inferiority; these individuals who are less likely to follow the rules of whiteness or to act upon racially conditioned attitudes, assumptions, and expectations are in a state of enlightened whiteness.

Below are the psychological impairments induced by attachment to the social construct of whiteness that are exhibited by those in blind, affirming, and toxic states of whiteness:

- Empathy deficit
- Distorted reality
- Anti-humanization/dehumanization
- Externalization of blame
- Anti-introspection
- Inhibited intellectual growth
- Irrationality (fear, resentment, anger, jealousy)
- Pathological defense mechanisms (acting out)
- Racially conditioned emotional needs

Blind Whiteness

- An empathy deficit is characteristic of this state because whiteness does not allow the individual to step outside of the racially centered white world to enter the world of the "other." Whiteness is accepted as normal and natural. An individual in this may be shocked by racist violence but detaches self from the other. An innocent black boy may have been shot by the police but there is no connection to him or the feelings of grief that his mother may be experiencing. "It is unfortunate, but these things just happen." This state is characterized by complacency and apathy.
- Externalization of blame may even occur because of years of indoctrination about the moral inferiority of blacks, especially of black males, externalization of blame may occur. Beliefs and feelings about the hoodie the black male was wearing, his attitude, or his

potential criminal behavior, even his size may be seen as the reason for the shooting rather than racism.

- Anti-introspection is characteristic of blind whiteness. There is no critical analysis of the concept of whiteness, undeserved advantage, the relationship between whiteness and racism. In this state the individual does not question religious beliefs about goodness to one's fellow man and the treatment of the other or the hypocrisy of the American creed related to liberty and justice for all.
- Stereotypes are accepted as facts; there is no questioning or critical analysis even when what was believed to be true is refuted by facts. This individual may regard blacks who achieve in areas previously thought reserved for white superiority to simply be individual exceptions.
- Another characteristic of anti-introspection is the inability to see people of color as individuals, grouping all together for the negative actions of one, never the positive acts. Individuals in the blind state of whiteness may even be very "liberal" in anti-racist expression and even actions, but takes great pride in whiteness. Often "does not see 'color.'"
- In the state of blind whiteness, an attachment to one's whiteness becomes one's total identity, esteem, and sense of status. Equal rights for blacks and black progress may be perceived as a loss of status. Inappropriate and irrational counterproductive guilt is related to white blindness. They may be overwhelmed to talk about race and racism.
- Unconscious or repression of dehumanizing comments or actions enables racism by "unseeing."

Inhibited Intellectual Growth

- In the blind state of whiteness, intellectual growth can be stalled. According to Dennis (1981), whiteness produces a mental poverty and inability to reflect from a sense of self. A particular consequence of racism is a counterpart of inhibition of intellectual growth. "Racism not only stalls and kills growth for individual whites, but also for the nation. Thus, the mental poverty that results from racism must inevitably create minds that are non-reflective, minds that indeed fear reflection."
- Whiteness decreases the ability of whites attached to the white identity to employ critical thinking and analysis. The distorted thinking of whiteness inhibits the ability to judge self and others or to perceive self and others accurately.
- Most critically, a dependency on whiteness and the inability to leave the comfort zone of whiteness inhibits the self-development, when whiteness is enough, self-actualization cannot occur. Because

blacks do not have the luxury of depending upon the privilege of whiteness, they are taught to work three to four times as hard to compete with less competent whites.

Perverse Whiteness

Perverse whiteness and toxic whiteness are fueled by the same set of racially conditioned needs. Irrational fears related to loss of "place" lead to the need to affirm one's whiteness through legal and extra-legal means. Those in the state of perverse whiteness conveniently and without conscience use the law or legal system, the "institutional power of whiteness" to harm or to murder blacks. Toxic whiteness, which will be discussed in the following paragraphs, is demonstrated by the use of extra-legal means such as racial terrorism, that is, the destruction of black communities and primarily through lynching.

- Perverse whiteness is expressed through deliberate and immoral actions designed to cause harm or have negative consequences for the intended victim. Black males are most usually the target of perverse whiteness. The power of institutional whiteness the legal system is the means by which the victim of the alleged offensive behavior is harmed. Deceit is most characteristic of this state of whiteness, as the individual is intentionally untruthful. Stereotypical images are relied upon to provoke the desired outcome. Injurious intent is carried out through fallacies, duplicitousness, illusions, and hoaxes. Actions taken in this state of whiteness are used for revenge, escape, or to cover for guilty actions.
- White women in a state of perverse whiteness have figured prominently in accusations that have led to the deaths of black males. A prime example is the case of fourteen-year-old Emmett Till who in 1955 was abducted, beaten, mutilated, shot, and his body sunk in the Tallahatchie River in Mississippi. Till was accused of offending a woman by allegedly whistling and flirting with Carolyn Bryant in the family's grocery store. Decades later, in 2008, Bryant disclosed that she had fabricated her testimony regarding her interaction with the boy.
- The racial hoax occurs when someone fabricates a crime and blames it on another person because of his/her race or an actual crime has been committed and the perpetrator falsely blames someone else based upon race. The stereotypical image of the black man as the criminal enables racial hoaxes to be committed against black men by whites in the perverse state of whiteness. Two incidents in particular demonstrate how effective the stereotypical image of the black male is in evoking actions toward them.

- In 1994, Susan Smith murdered her two children, a three-year-old and a fourteen-month-old, both boys. She falsely claimed that a black man had kidnapped her sons during a carjacking. Months later, she confessed to letting her car roll into the lake, drowning her sons. Her motivation for the hoax was to facilitate a relationship with a wealthy man; however, she deliberately and wantonly placed the lives of innocent black men in danger.
- In 1989, Charles Stuart lied saying that a black gunman forced his way into the car and shot him and murdered his wife. Stuart even picked an innocent black man, Willie Bennett, from a photo lineup. It was revealed that Stuart had murdered his own wife in order to cash in on his wife's insurance policy. The criminal stereotype of the black male enabled the false statements of Stuart to initially be believed by law enforcement.
- The most recent and blatant expression of perverse whiteness occurred in 2020, when Amy Cooper, a white woman, called the police on a black man, Christian Cooper, in Central Park. On a videotape, Cooper says, "I'm going to tell them there's an African American man threatening my life." The perpetrator relied upon institutional whiteness the force of the law to get even with a black man whom she felt had offended her or gotten "out of his place."
- A preponderance of actions related to perverse whiteness have occurred in 2020. Whites have called the police on blacks cashing a pay check, taking a phone call in a hotel lobby, golfing too slowly, working out in a gym, barbecuing in a park, moving into an apartment, as well as not waving while leaving an Airbnb accommodation. "Living while black" is the name given to these expressions of perverse whiteness.

Toxic Whiteness

Toxic whiteness is blind whiteness accompanied by fear, anger, resentment, jealousy, and hatred. Toxic whiteness is characterized by an irrational fear of losing privilege, of being powerless; anxiety can occur even in middle-class status. One's sense of self becomes externally focused, on the black, because "being better than a n-----" is the only way that one can derive status. Toxic whiteness most often is the overt racism and violence that most American whites consider to be "racist."

Irrationality (Fears, Resentment, Anger)

- Toxic whiteness is characterized by irrational obsession with blacks—what are "they" getting? At my expense? What am I losing—and irrational concern with Affirmative Action progress made by blacks. Irrational anger, jealousy, resentment, and hatred are triggered by blacks refusing to stay in their prescribed "place" in society or making progress that is not felt deserved by blacks. Those in a state of toxic whiteness may have experienced previous oppression related to classism and use displacement as a defense mechanism.

Dehumanization

- Toxic whiteness turns individuals into moral monsters; those engaging in acts which dehumanize the victim dehumanize themselves as well. They are inflamed by racist sentiments, grievances, and passions. Toxic whiteness is most often characterized by pathological fears and anxieties related to loss of social status. According to John Ordway, "the paranoid racist lives with constant fear."
- The fear of loss of place is key to the subhuman violence committed against blacks by whites. Putting blacks in their place was such a significant and symbolic event. Resentment toward black progress has been a catalyst for the murdering of black citizens and the burning of black communities, for example, Tulsa, Oklahoma (1921). Independence on the part of blacks could not be tolerated because it refuted the myth of white supremacy.
- Toxic whiteness is characterized by dehumanization or subhuman acts. The dehumanization of whites occurs through the dehumanization of others by engaging in subhuman acts. Dehumanization through violence validates toxic whiteness. Examples include the torture, lynching, and murder of Claude Neale. Neale's 1943 murder was advertised in the press and attended by thousands, including families and children. In the picnic atmosphere Neale was tortured, forced to eat his genitals, and portions of his charred and brutalized body were taken as souvenirs. Putting blacks in their place was such a significant and symbolic event. Young white boys through their participation in such violent actions are learning about how to preserve white power (DuRocher, 2011).
- A delusional sense of power or control is experienced by those in a state of toxic whiteness when they are able to denigrate a black. During the Jim Crow era, feelings of power and esteem came from forcing a black off of the sidewalk. Today, microaggressions, that is, insinuating a black only has a job because of Affirmative Action, deliberately sabotaging black efforts in the educational system or the workplace, provide a sense of power for those in a state of toxic whiteness.
- Toxic whiteness includes rage toward any white who disavows whiteness or does not abide by the rules of whiteness. The rage may be expressed as ostracism, labeling as a race traitor or Communist, or even death as in the case of individuals the likes of Viola

Liuzzo, Andrew Goodman, and Michael Schwerner, civil rights activists murdered in Mississippi.

- Toxic whiteness may also be demonstrated toward non-whites through vehement opposition to black acknowledgment of black achievement, as well as the promotion policies and practices that exploit, or physically harm non-whites and their communities.
- Toxic whiteness through thoughts, speech, and actions (directly or indirectly) maintain the white supremacy culture.
- Class shame was and is often an element of toxic whiteness expressed as resentment toward black progress. "Why him and not me? Why am I poor and struggling and he has a large home and two cars? Why is he a prosperous farmer rather than struggling like myself?' How can a black be doing better in America than me? He is too independent, too uppity, who does he think he is?" Related to class shame is the externalization of blame; rather than working harder to improve their own lot, one in toxic whiteness resorts to community-sanctioned violence against individual and black communities.

Pathological Defense Mechanisms are utilized in blind and toxic whiteness.

Delany (1970) suggests common pathological defense mechanisms: "acting out," commonly combined with projection, which involves ascribing to others the behaviors, thoughts, feelings, and attitudes that they have themselves but which they find unacceptable and hence attribute to others; depersonalization, which is the denial of the reality that the act involves another human; and justification. Ascribing to black men immoral and sociopathic behaviors in the image of the stereotypic Brute has provided a license to kill innocent black youth such as Trayvon Martin and Michael Brown who were perceived to be hoodlums and demons.

ENLIGHTENED "WHITENESS"

Those in an enlightened state of whiteness have the ability to think constructively about whiteness and race—an awareness of how whites are manipulated by racism—resist prevailing racial attitudes of white superiority and black inferiority. They are open to seeking accurate information, asking questions, and examining the lives of non-whites in American society. Enlightened whiteness is an identity and sense of esteem that is not focused on being white.

- Enlightened whiteness involves critical self-reflection and questioning the concept of whiteness. Enlightened whiteness does not believe in unearned privilege.

- Enlightened whiteness is the experience of empathy and compassion for those who are the victims of racial oppression. Enlightened whiteness is respecting and appreciating racial and ethnic differences. Enlightened whiteness sees people of color as individuals rather than a group. Enlightened whiteness involves the efforts to bring unconscious stereotypes to a conscious level so that they can be confronted, challenged, and changed.
- Enlightened whiteness is productive and responsible, committed to doing anything possible to resist white supremacy ideology and heal racism in the society.
- Enlightened whiteness is often expressed in childhood. As children they are troubled by and unable to accept racist indoctrination. Lillian Smith (1970) provides an excellent example of enlightened whiteness. At an early age, she questioned what she was taught about race and the "ritual of segregation":
  - "My first concern with it [segregation] was because it affected me, not because it affected Negroes."
  - "I did not like being restricted to members of the white race." "I secretly attached myself [to my colored friends]."
  - "Everything was contradicting everything else, and I knew it." "This separation was different; it could be changed."

CONCLUSION

To break the cycle of generational indoctrination into white supremacy culture, individual whites will have to enter into a state of enlightened whiteness. Institutions must take deliberate steps to present a counternarrative and create a counterculture to that of white supremacy. The generational indoctrination of white supremacy in which the tenets of disconnection, separation, and lack of empathy toward blacks and other people of color were encouraged has seeped into the whole of American society so that in the present day, all students regardless of skin color are victims of bullying and violence. Educational institutions have an obligation to be the leading force in breaking the cycle of white supremacy.

> "White people cannot in the generality be taken as models of how to live.
> Rather the white man is himself in some need of standards,
> which will release him from his confusion and place him once again
> in the fruitful communication with the depths of his own being."

—James Baldwin, *The Fire Next Time*

SIX

The Promise and Limits of "Whiteness"

Indentured servants, the first group to be indoctrinated into white supremacist ideology, were particularly vulnerable to the viral nature of white supremacy because of their low sense of self; they were servants to other whites and treated poorly; they were hurt by class oppression. Generations of common whites, as they were called by the elite class, were and still are as wounded by classism as ever and depend upon their "whiteness," given to them by the elites to make them feel a sense of worth. They are now conditioned by racism—the practice of white supremacy ideology—to meet their emotional needs.

President Lyndon B. Johnson stated it more succinctly:

> If you can convince the lowest white man he's better than the best colored man, he won't notice you're picking his pocket. Hell, give him somebody to look down on, and he'll empty his pockets for you.

In this chapter, we will examine the appeal and power of whiteness to those who had experienced the limits of whiteness. The social control of whites through racism was evidenced by two factors in particular, fear mongering by the demagogues, and meeting the emotional needs of a stigmatized group. The social construct of "whiteness" is a powerful psychological tool used to control those who had suffered class degradation and dehumanization. Whiteness provides a mechanism for the three major human needs of belongingness/affiliation, self-worth/value, and power/control.

THE AMERICAN DREAM

The promise of white supremacy ideology was that those designated and perceived to be white would enjoy freedom of movement, white advantage, and most critically the opportunity to pursue and achieve the American dream. However, historians have failed to provide an accurate and broad history of how class differences in particular played and continue to play a part in which whites fully enjoy "whiteness." There are reasons for this failure.

Two factors refuted the ideology of white supremacy and white superiority during the antebellum South. First was the presence of free blacks, some of which prospered, the other was the presence of landless, dependent, and poverty-stricken whites who presented a major problem for the ruling class. Some free blacks had come to own farms and were residents of self-supporting enclaves. The ruling class took steps to resolve the issue by removing free blacks from states such as North Carolina and Mississippi.

For generations, the message of white superiority and supremacy had been instilled in the collective white mind. This was a paradoxical message however for five million poor southern whites. In the class-oriented planter society of the antebellum South, white skin in itself was not enough to secure all of the privileges of whiteness. Poor whites lived and suffered at the bottom of the antebellum social structure, oppressed in their own special way.

Poor whites were those who were landless and owned no slaves. This population also included "common" whites who could have been employed as mechanics (those who traveled from place to place taking odd jobs), laborers, tenant farmers, artisans, clerks, petty shopkeepers, small farmers, plantation overseers, squatters, or those who fished and hunted for subsistence. In the few decades leading up to the Civil War, poor whites comprised approximately one-third of the population of the antebellum Deep South. They had few opportunities to overcome their economic condition.

Enslaved African Americans were considered three-fifths of a human. This was decreed for political purposes only; they were at the very bottom of America's social hierarchy; they were chattel, only a fraction of a person. The racialized slavery of the black-skinned gave a cache of whiteness to poor whites that took on an ideological meaning; it carried no financial benefit or social standing.

Thandeka (2000) describes the poor white man, like black slaves, as being racial victims of the upper class, however, poor whites were not conscious of their victimhood. The poor white lived in a "class illusion" which separated him from the actual experience of his life. The poor whites' vanity was thus based on both fact and illusion. The fact pertained to the poor white's race, but the illusion pertained to their class status.

TREATMENT OF POOR WHITES

> "The lords of the lash are not only absolute masters of the blacks, who are bought and sold, and driven about like so many cattle, but they are also the oracles and arbiters of all non-slaveholding whites, whose freedom is merely nominal, and whose unparallel degradation is purposely and fiendishly perpetuated."
> —Hinton Helper, *The Impending Crisis of the South: How to Meet It*, 1857

Slavery did not benefit the common white man; in fact, it worked to his economic detriment. Poor whites had to compete against unpaid slave labor, working for low wages when work was available. Black enslavement decreased the need for white labor and white tenants.

Black enslavement created a large underclass of whites who either could not find work or found work that never paid a livable wage. Poor whites, unable to purchase land, lived in the filth, starvation, and ignorance of extreme poverty. The treatment of poor whites foreshadowed the brutal and violent treatment that blacks would endure after Emancipation.

Many of the stereotypes held of enslaved African Americans were attributed to poor whites: they were considered ignorant, lazy, filthy, promiscuous, violent, and the product of their bad ancestry—indentured servants, vagabonds, and criminals brought to America during the colonial period. Because of the number of landless and non-slave-owning whites, the elites eventually saw them as a threat to the security of the southern way of life, and imposed social control measures such as imposed ignorance, a criminal justice system with only them in mind, and extra-legal activities taken by the ruling class against them.

The planter class would not support a public education system even as they strictly controlled the flow of information to this group through censorship laws and persuasive racial appeals. The total economic hardship of poor, landless whites ensured their continued uneducated lives— they were the least likely group to send their children to schools.

Poor whites were incarcerated for nonviolent crimes such as trading, drinking, and other social interaction with enslaved and free blacks. The state of Mississippi built a state penitentiary which became another weapon in their arsenal to discipline "unruly whites" who challenged racial boundaries. Slave patrols were used to control the behavior of landless whites as well as enslaved blacks. In some cases, landless whites were represented in the patrols even as they were distrusted, feared that unsupervised themselves, they would not maintain racial and class boundaries of the area's slave society.

The ruling planter class made upward mobility impossible for poor whites. Competition with unpaid labor, the inability to acquire land, forced ignorance, and the criminal justice system kept poor whites in a marginalized state. When land became available in the 1830s, the prices were too expensive for poor whites. Additionally, politicians made it even more of an obstacle to acquire land with the passage of the Specie Circular Act of 1836. Merritt (2017) contends that the Specie Circular Act helped to further solidify class distinctions as the law required that all government land purchases had to be transacted in silver or gold. Poor whites were at a clear disadvantage.

The 1840s continued with the economic misfortunes of the small land-owners in the form of bankruptcy and foreclosure, which allowed plantation owners to purchase larger tracts of land. The situation grew worse with the cotton boom of the 1850s. The richest slaveholders grew their wealth, the non-slaveholders continued to flounder, increasingly shut out of the market economy.

Lands opening up in the West seemed to hold possibilities to create social equality among whites of all classes, since landholding was a key to higher social status, but few landless whites from the south had the capital to even buy a wagon to head west, let alone buy any land.

As in the colonial era, when the ruling elite prevented indentured servants freed from their bondage from acquiring land, the power of the planter class kept the best and largest tracts of lands in their own hands. The southern elites used their political power to prevent the passage of the Homestead Act of 1862, which would have allowed poor whites an opportunity to acquire land.

BIRACIAL ALLIANCES

During the late antebellum era, the planter elite again began to fear a class alliance between poor whites and enslaved and free African Americans. Most troubling to the planter class were the relationships that existed between these landless, non-slaveholding whites and enslaved and free blacks. These alliances included trade networks, socializing (especially drinking), and sleeping together.

Divide and control was the method of choice during the antebellum days as it had been in the colonial era. Lockley (2001) writes about an attempt that was made to create animosity between landless whites and African Americans. "Slaveholders often encouraged an attitude of contempt for 'poor white trash' among their slaves, while simultaneously subscribing to a definition of freedom and independence based on race to whites. In addition, the elite began to make social distinctions between the two groups, and to ferment racial hatred in the workplace."

The planter class placed tighter restrictions on the enslaved, reducing opportunities for biracial contact. And the elite sent a clear message to the poorest members of white society that the threat biracial interaction posed to Southern society would no longer be tolerated. In many areas, one of the primary duties of the slave patrol was more to keep slaves isolated from poor whites to prevent clandestine transactions and other unsanctioned activities than to look for runaways.

Fearmongering, however, was the most potent tool used to keep landless and non-slaveholding whites ignorant and controlled. Landless non-slaveholding whites had no personal or economic interest in the slave system; however, slaveholders used every possible method to convince them to support secession and slavery. They used insidious racist propaganda to stoke the fears related to freed blacks:

- Poor white's wages would fall quickly and drastically to the point of literal starvation.
- Poor whites would be the social equals of newly freed blacks.
- A bloody race war between the two impoverished classes would follow after freedom and poor whites would be slaughtered by the thousands.
- Without the means to flee the South, the poor white man would encounter the "ravages of the black plague."
- Freedom for blacks meant that Negro domination and amalgamation would follow.

The fear of loss of status, of being no better than the enslaved was engrained in the minds of plain and poor whites in the Confederate states and some border states. If slavery ended, poor whites were convinced that blacks would be their equals and they would no longer be superior. This need to feel superior, a belief in white supremacy, encouraged those with no self-interest to delude themselves that they had a stake in preserving the slave system. Poor whites and yeoman farmers were convinced to fight for the interest of the slaveholders for several reasons, some material, but most critically psychological. Some were convinced that slavery would keep their families safe, others looked forward to a steady wage, while others feeling a sense of powerlessness thought it was in their best interest to align with the planter class.

Keri Leigh Merritt, author and historian (2017), writes that through identifying with whiteness and supporting the interests of the planter class, "Poor white men, who had spent most of their lives without a sense of honor, finally found a way to feel valued by their society. By protecting their homes, families, and communities, poor whites were able to elevate their social status. Any threat to white racist pride could thereafter never go unchallenged." After the loss of the war, poor whites, still impoverished but taught very skillfully to be in fear of social equality with blacks, remained devoted to the racial caste system, fueled on by the wealthy elite of the South.

Historical evidence provides insight as to what the primal fear of the ruling class has and continues to be. It might be reasonably inferred from the pattern of social control imposed since the Colonial Era that the major fear of the ruling class is of the common white man. Social control methods employed during the Colonial Era, the antebellum era, and after Emancipation directly affected common whites. The most destructive element of the racial demagoguery that occurred was the fear and hatred that remained in the consciousness of whites. The fear, anger, and resentment toward blacks encouraged a torrent of racial violence that included lynching, beatings, and the destruction of property and entire black communities.

CLASS TENSION

Class tensions between the common white man and the planter class came to the forefront as the Civil War drew closer. The planter class's desire to secede from the Union to preserve black slavery increased tensions between the two classes. Landless and non-slaveholding whites had nothing to gain from seceding from the Union. They wanted nothing to do with secession and had very little interest in fighting for the Confederacy. While they initially resisted the southern cause, military inscription, impressment, and the confiscation of whatever personal property the poor white had made the Confederate army an option that was hard to refuse; they were an unwilling force of poor folks.

The war protected the interests of the elites as property owners and slaveowners. While wealthy planters continued to plant cotton, small farmers were forced to grow food stuffs for the troops. What was considered most unfair by the foot soldiers was that planters who owned twenty or more slaves were excused from the draft. In April 1862, the Confederate Congress passed a military conscription act and poor men were forced to fight.

Poor whites deserted in great numbers, their rallying cry, "It is a rich man's war." By 1864, Jefferson Davis had to admit that "two-thirds" of the fighting men were absent. The resentment toward the planter elite and the war was so intense that deserters formed guerilla bands or gangs and attacked government supply trains, burned bridges, and raided plantations.

According to Merritt (2017), it was "the plight of poor whites helped push the slaveholders to secession from the Union, and their active resistance or their passive non-compliance added to the Confederate military problem. The Confederacy lost the war at least in part because of the number of poor white desertions from the Confederate army."

The fears of the elite whites that their slaves would get together with common whites and overthrow the system of enslavement suffered by both groups were never brought to fruition. Landless, non-slaveholding whites were more of an annoyance than a real threat to the institution of slavery. Ultimately, race consciousness overpowered class consciousness in the minds of the poor whites, and the ideology of white supremacy prevailed. The promise of whiteness, the feeling of superiority, social mobility, and expectation to achieve the American dream was and is a powerful enticement.

Bolton (1994) states that if "economic losers" had united in opposition to the South's ruling class that they could have posed a formidable danger to the institution of slavery. However, no such sustained or coordinated attach from the antebellum South's lower classes ever occurred. He suggests that racism played the pivotal role in driving a wedge between whites and blacks in the end.

That fear of the elite since the Colonial Era, during the Antebellum Era, and magnified during and after Emancipation is the fear of a biracial alliance of those occupying very similar low positions in the American social hierarchy. While most whites, to a degree, have the advantages associated with white skin, class status intervenes and prevents the experience of whiteness by the poor working class, and many whites who consider themselves to be middle class.

THE PSYCHOLOGICAL POWER OF "WHITENESS"

The social construction of whiteness has both ideological and psychological appeal. The Declaration of Independence promises to property-owning white males the advantages of life, liberty, and the pursuit of happiness (while poor whites, non-whites, and females were ignored). The privileges of a life without fear of personal safety and security, the right of social mobility, and through hard work and the spirit of individualism, the achievement of the American dream.

It is, however, the psychological appeal of whiteness that is most powerful, especially for whites who were stigmatized by low social status. Attachment to "whiteness" provides whites not belonging to the elite class a sense of belonging, self-worth, hope, and control. The true power of whiteness lies in meeting the emotional needs of those who have been degraded and oppressed by a lower social status. To be white was to be free, independent, and able to pursue opportunities only available to those with white skin. This was a fantasy; however, the poor whites believed it and knew it was better than blackness which meant true bondage and dependency, not realizing that this was basically their lot in life also.

European society was a class-based society. Kings were believed to have been divinely appointed. The power and wealth that they enjoyed came directly from their connection to God. To be psychologically aligned with the master was the most potent power a bondservant of European ancestry could possess. Belonging and connection to the masterclass based on skin color was a brilliant powerful psychological trick that was strategically employed by the ruling class. Racism is the tool that solidifies those designated as white in this society regardless of class position.

Evidence of the class degradation and dehumanizing treatment of "poor whites" suggests that they would take any actions to avoid the humiliation of lower-class whiteness. The stigmatization and dehumanization toward the group, which included incarceration, violence, and denial of education, foreshadowed the treatment of blacks freed by Emancipation. Whiteness was an illusion of freedom from class degradation for lower class whites and a sense of belonging to the same class by skin color and affiliation with the ruling class.

"Whiteness" was a very powerful antidote to the previous feelings of anger and resentment toward the planter class. To be better than blacks with whom they shared the same economic conditions, but about whom they received the paradoxical indoctrination of white superiority, brought a sense of self-worth and value to poor whites. Whiteness and white racial belonging gave lower class and poor whites a sense of hope, independence, and choice they had never experienced before, the hope as a white man of finally having the opportunity to achieve prosperity and become one of the elite class. With blacks firmly on the bottom of the social hierarchy, lower class whites were finally able to enjoy whiteness.

The greatest power of whiteness and racism as social control resulted in the willingness of whites to unite in race rather than class consciousness with poor blacks like themselves. In December 1865, half a million poor whites faced starvation. The major help for all impoverished persons came from the Bureau of Refugees, Freedmen, and Abandoned Lands, established by Congress in March 1865. The propaganda fed into the minds of whites was so effective that poor whites rejected such programs as "nigger programs" and consequently suffered disease, ignorance, and poverty. Operating against their own group self-interest, poor whites even refused to attend the schools created by the bureau.

At the end of Reconstruction, whiteness was again useful to the power elite as a social control mechanism to insure white political control. Common white folk were urged to identify against a race rather than with a class, their very own class, not the upper white class. Fearmongering was used to convince common whites that if whites split over political or economic matters, blacks would hold the balance of power and would institute Negro rule. In reality, the emotional appeal of whiteness created a system of social control that caused the economic, political, and social status of poor whites to deteriorate. The same rules, such as poll taxes that prohibited black participation in the political process applied to poor whites as well; again, full participation in white privilege was restricted by class status.

Appealing to the sense of identity and esteem for common whites were Black Codes and Jim Crow laws. Designed to keep whites and blacks totally separate, Jim Crow laws were effective in also providing whites stigmatized by class status the experience of feeling self-worth and power. To be able to go into a restroom in which a black was denied or to drink from a white drinking fountain provided a sense of power and superiority. While they enjoyed these white privileges, common whites were unaware of the intentions of the racist laws; segregation was designed to prevent the type of biracial alliances that had occurred during the late antebellum period.

Racial violence, especially in the form of lynching, was a masterful manipulation to meet the emotional needs of both upper- and lower-class whites in a variety of ways. Lynching served the motives of those in power through havoc and control. It reinforced identification with whiteness and served to bond whites regardless of class differences. Lynching was a way to help ease class tension within white supremacy; it minimized social and class distinctions between upper- and lower-class whites. Poor whites were able to experience a racial power that contradicted the inferiority of their class position. The more horrific and subhuman the act of violence, the greater sense of power and control experienced.

THE IMPACT OF RACISM UPON WHITES

The racism and inequality produced by stereotypical indoctrination is a mechanism for both economic and social control of whites as well as blacks. While blacks bear the brunt of racial inequality, racism also hurts whites in so many economic and political ways. Using economic research, Reich (1981) found evidence that racial inequality hurts white workers. Specifically, Reich found that:

- Racial inequality exacerbates inequality among whites because racial inequality diminishes the capacity of workers—blacks and whites together!—to organize in solidarity, thus weakening the labor movement and hurting most white as well as black workers and thereby reducing the total income share of labor.
- Racial antagonisms deflect attention from labor grievances relating to working conditions, enabling employers to cut costs without a substantial decline in worker productivity.

Racial inequality increases inequality among whites by benefiting high-income whites and by hurting most whites. A shocking example of the control of white beliefs, attitudes, and actions related to governmental assistance is revealed in surveys in which whites responded to items related to social services—welfare, food stamps, and Medicaid. In the collective white mind, blacks are the largest share of those receiving government assistance, which makes the whites vehemently oppose white taxpayer money going to pay for undeserving blacks. The truth is that working-class whites are the biggest beneficiaries of federal poverty reduction programs.

Research indicates that whites make up the largest share of Americans receiving food stamps—36.2 percent compared to 25.6 percent black, and Medicaid 43 percent compared to 18 percent black (Delaney and Edwards-Levy, 2018).

The mythology of whiteness deludes working- and middle-class whites. It manipulates them into believing that fewer numbers of whites using the services indicates a moral superiority and that whites hold to the American value of individualism in which each person takes care of themselves, and does not depend upon others. Working- and middle-class whites vote against their own self-interests and those of their families when they agree with ruling class politicians that cuts to government spending, especially social and educational programs, are necessary.

Physician Jonathan Metzl's alarming 2019 book, *Dying of Whiteness*, dramatically illustrates the pervasive and persistent control of the ideology of whiteness. According to him, the two historical stereotypes of black laziness and violence are so embedded in the collective white mind that choices made are destructive to the health and well-being of middle- and working-class whites: "Investment in a sense of whiteness ironically harms the aggregate well-being of U.S. whites as a demographic group, thereby making whiteness itself a negative health indicator."

This group votes against its own material and biological self-interest by disdaining federal monies they believe are meant for blacks. They are against Medicaid expansion because they fear white tax dollars will go toward lazy minorities, even as they suffer from inadequate and restricted access to healthcare.

The stereotypical image of the Brute, the violent black male, again created after Emancipation and during Reconstruction, continues to control the beliefs, attitudes, and actions of whites. Metzl (2019) cites an opinion study published in the journal PLOS ONE found that attitudes toward guns retained by many US whites appear to be influenced by illogical racial biases related to the fear of black violence and crime. He states further that "legal historians place white anxieties about control of the black population at the center of the gun debate. As this debate continues, white men comprise the majority of gun suicide victims in the

United States, a mental health issue." The rules of whiteness appear to make the identity a formation worth fighting and dying for.

There is the conventional belief that a class system does not exist in the United States. This point of view is totally false. Racism in the United States is the "sledgehammer" used to preserve the class system. Since the founding of the nation, one's class has been a determining factor in one's ability to fully experience "whiteness" and achieve the American dream. Racism has been the mechanism used to distract attention from white class manipulation, exploitation, and oppression. Classism is a system by which one's freedom is limited.

The delusion of white superiority combined with class-based oppression creates a sense of powerlessness especially in white males. Class-based powerlessness produces feelings ranging from insecurity to frustration, inferiority, and shame. Class-based powerlessness can lead to greater attachment to whiteness despite the obvious inability to *ever* attain all the privileges of whiteness, to be fully white. The failure to achieve the American dream of wealth and power promised by whiteness can also result in psychopathic racial behavior. The anger, resentment, and hatred resulting from a perceived loss of place has been the cause of sanctioned violence to put blacks back in their designated place in society for way too many days, years, centuries.

Classism can pose a heavy burden on whites. "What happens to the dignity men see in themselves and in each other, when their freedom is checked by class?" ask Sennett and Cobb (1993). "Whiteness" cannot protect them from the feeling of getting nowhere despite one's efforts when contrasted with those of a higher social class and even blacks. This sense of powerlessness can create feelings of inadequacy and even personal resentment.

"There is considerable evidence for example," according to Bennett (1970), "that the culture's stress on success and status induces exaggerated anxieties and fears which are displaced onto the area of race relations." Bennett asserts that particularly among low and middle-income whites that prejudice is "an avenue of flight, a cry of help from desperate men stifling in the prisons of their skins." He suggests that repeated studies have shown that hatred of the Negro is associated as "a socially sanctioned outlet for personal and social anxieties and frustrations."

One of America's best kept secrets, asserts Zweig (2000), is that the great majority of Americans are of working-class status. "Class is involved in the issues that have dominated economic and political life in the United States over the last quarter of the twentieth century . . . the issue has played out in a way that has strengthened the power of the capitalist class, degraded the life of the working class, and caught the working class in the middle." Yet white Americans continue to be controlled by racist images and language. All thoughts of class consciousness and alliance with those in the same economic and social conditions but with different skin color have been obliterated.

In a state of blind whiteness, whites never consider that from the colonial times, the antebellum days, to current times that the ruling class operate as a collective in getting their will. A group of colonial aristocrats made it more difficult for freed bond servants to buy land; a group of southern planters kept whites impoverished during the enslavement period. Today, groups of investors and well-placed politicians make decisions about how government monies will be spent. The success and wealth made through "rugged individualism" is something that most working-class white Americans today will never see.

Establishing class consciousness in middle- and working-class whites and uniting whites and blacks against their joint economic exploitation has been destroyed at every turn. Racist demagoguery has sabotaged all efforts. In only two cases, enlightened whiteness appeared to make a headway against racism.

First, during the Populist movement which began in the early 1890s, it appeared that a biracial coalition of farmers could work together to bring about agrarian reform. Racist propaganda, however, created fear in poor white farmers that blacks would become their social equals. The commitment to class consciousness, the awareness of their own social position in white society, and most critically, the psychological threat of social equality for blacks doomed the movement and prevented poor whites from freeing themselves from economic exploitation by the powerful elite class.

Secondly, in what might be called the first "Rainbow Coalition," a group of poor white youth in Chicago in the early 1960s, "The Young Patriots," children of white Appalachians who had come North during the Great Migration, joined with the Black Panthers and Young Lords (Latinos) in a multiracial coalition to better the lives of poor residents of Chicago. Under the leadership of Black Panther Fred Hampton, this multiracial group established breakfast programs for children, free health clinics, and organized tenants to demand fixes to their buildings. This coalition based on class interests served the poor of each community.

When Fred Hampton was assassinated, the old racist technique of divide and conquer instantly appeared to inspire fear and distrust. Rumors were spread that members of the Young Patriots were members of the Ku Klux Klan and that blacks were planning to take over the white neighborhood. For a brief moment, these groups achieved class-based power.

CONCLUSION

W. E. B. Du Bois, in *Black Reconstruction in America,* argued that whiteness served as a "public and psychological wage" that provided poor whites in the nineteenth and early twentieth centuries a social status that increased their sense of well-being despite material or economic gain. This psychological compensation has continued to be a significant force in determining working-class white's perception of their identity, status, and esteem.

The fear of the loss of racial status remains as potent today as it was during the Civil War era and not only among poor whites. The myth of white superiority and the racial pride it produces is part of the collective identity and esteem of many white Americans. For many whites, the fears are overwhelming as America faces what is described as the "browning" of America, the loss of a white majority population, "replacement" and declining "assumed" superior status.

While Americans, including white Americans, voted for Barack Obama to become president of the United States, the black face in the White House brought on old fears of loss of racial status and the privilege of whiteness. Many white Americans today, through more outward acts of prejudice and racism, are exhibiting the same fears as those yeomen farmers and poor whites more than 150 years ago.

What is not recognized or allowed to be brought to their conscious awareness is that these fears are created and perpetuated to maintain ruling class supremacy. It is the middle- and working-class white that has always posed the major problem for the ruling class. And it is the middle and working class which have proven to be such a supremely easy group to control; their beliefs, attitudes, and behaviors are not really theirs; they were culturally conditioned generations ago.

Increasingly however, as "whiteness" fails during harsh economic times such as the COVID-19 pandemic, working-class whites are pessimistic about the future and the ability to achieve the promised American dream. Graham (2017) reports that "increasing mortality rates among uneducated middle-aged whites which are driven by suicide, drug addiction, and alcohol poisoning are clear markers of desperation and lack of hope." She states further that these trends reflect a drop in perceived status of low-skilled white workers. The "distorted reality" produced by whiteness has prevented working-class whites in particular from developing the resilience and the skills that blacks and other people of color found necessary to survive in the American society.

Racism manipulates middle-class, working-class, and poor whites into believing in and supporting an ideological superiority, while they in most cases do not benefit materially. Without material gain, common

whites are actually only defending the myth of white supremacy. Whiteness keeps common whites focused on the place of blacks and prevents
them for looking realistically at their class position.

SEVEN

The Time for Change

A vaccine is the organism's most potent protection against infection from a virus. To save a society that has been infected with a destructive and devastating virus, a vaccine is desperately needed.

It is painfully apparent that it is time a vaccine be developed to prevent the further infection of the collective white American mind with the virus of whiteness and white supremacy, with the spread of the infectious virus of racism that has dehumanized white Americans in the same way it has dehumanized America's citizens of color. It is time for change.

> "It is time for white people to release themselves from their own captivity."
>
> —James Baldwin

Historically, pandemics have explosively disturbed the core of economic, social, and cultural structure of impacted societies. America will never be the same after the COVID-19 pandemic, for with the force of an earthquake, it has torn open and exposed the impact of the racist and classist underpinnings of America's economic system, institutions, and culture. Just as the coronavirus will remain in the organs of those affected, for generations the virus of white supremacy ideology has remained in the collective mind and spirit of America.

Americans have been unable to fight off the deleterious effects of the racist demagoguery that has influenced the beliefs, values, attitudes, perceptions, and behavior of white Americans. But it is time for change. It is time for those Americans who identify as and are perceived as white to free themselves of the virus of white superiority that has been driven into the collective American mind since the European indentured servants were first infected with it.

The coronavirus has revealed the pervasiveness of white supremacy ideology and its impact not only on people of color, those most ravaged by the virus, but the vulnerability of white Americans as well depending upon their social and economic status in society. The value system of individualism, a core tenet of white supremacy is no longer applicable as Americans of all colors file for unemployment benefits, fear eviction from their homes and wait in lines for food to feed their families. Ultimately the coronavirus is a test of the white supremacy ideology that has prevailed throughout American culture.

The urgency and the force of the pandemic created a "pause" from the normality of American life and the need for Americans to quarantine and "cocoon" in their homes. Unable to go to work, send children to school, carry on life as usual, they spent their first days receiving a continuous flow of news from the networks and internet. During this early period, the bubble of whiteness was burst, and white Americans came face-to-face with killings of innocent African Americans followed by protests against systematic racism and police brutality. White Americans, especially the young, joined the chorus demanding social justice in the nation.

Protesters challenged the adoration of figures, especially from the former Confederate States of America, representing and embodying white supremacist ideals. Long-standing corporate, sports, and other institutions began to examine their policies and practices.

The cocooning of Americans created a period that has been unequaled in American life and culture. The civil rights movement from its beginning to its end with the signing of the Fair Housing Act in 1968, garnered support from "enlightened" whites. But it did not force the nation as a whole to reflect on its racist history. This space in 2020 offered Americans a time to pause, to reflect, and to change. We have begun again as the nation of our ideals, a nation where "all" of its citizens truly have freedom and equal opportunity to pursue the American dream. The coronavirus space offered the opportunity for Americans to:

- find out who we really are as a nation;
- reflect on the reality of American life for all of its citizens;
- emerge from the bubble of whiteness;
- develop a sense of empathy and compassion for those oppressed because of skin color or social condition;
- look critically at America to examine the myths of a post-racial and classless society;
- see America from a different angle or vision;
- see real American life for blacks, browns, the poor;
- focus on and acknowledge the contradictions between American ideals and the reality of American life in terms of race and class;
- imagine America differently;
- realize the importance of essential workers in society, regardless of race or class; and

- consider a new American identity based on stated ideals and promises; a virtuous America.

THE IMPACT OF WHITE SUPREMACY IDEOLOGY

White supremacy ideology and the creation of "whiteness" created a culture of racial distrust, resentment, hatred, and violence while perpetuating a rigid class system which keeps many working-class and poor whites at the margins. Racism, the product of the creation of "whiteness," is a mechanism for maintaining the economic status quo.

The "old" American culture undergirded by white supremacy ideology:

- promotes racial and class divisions;
- prevents the telling and oppresses the documentation and publishing of the true American history;
- keeps Americans in a perpetual state of denial;
- damages the moral fiber of the American people;
- hurts the well-being of most needy Americans;
- fosters hypocrisy in terms of stated ideals and social realities; and
- harms America's prestige and standing in the world.

CHANGE FOR AMERICA

Change is a process of unfolding, transformation; releasing what was. For America, change has many elements. Change is accepting the reality that the coronavirus has exposed. Change means releasing old belief and value systems based upon the ideology of white supremacy. Change means the expression of a new narrative to guide the nation from the highest levels of government and embodied by all institutions. Change means being open to a new vision of America, a society that works for "all" of the people. Change is the shedding of a consciousness of separation, division, and exclusion and embracing connection, oneness, and inclusiveness. Most crucially for America, change will mean freeing ourselves from white supremacy.

There have been other eras and opportunities to change the beliefs and values that undergird American culture: Reconstruction, the return of African American veterans after World War I and II, the civil rights movement, rebellions in American cities. Laws and moral appeals did not change the American mind. Some change did occur during and after these events, but core beliefs and values of white supremacy ideology were more vigorously promoted. As a result, because racism was not regarded as a moral issue and the inherent structure of white supremacy ideology was not acknowledged, confronted, or challenged, the ideology was reinforced and perpetuated in America.

As a result of the COVID-19 pandemic, however, American ideals and its contradictions have been brought to the forefront. At a deeper level, the consciousness of America has been disturbed, thus providing an opening to question, reflect, and examine core beliefs and values as well as their impact on the well-being of all citizens. It has made us come face to face with the mythologies that define us as a nation. The economic, social, and cultural impact of the corona virus demands a return to and completion of the journey toward embracing and practicing American ideals. This is such an opportunity for the nation to be that of its highest calling.

The greatest obstacle to this change will be the ideas or beliefs held as truth that lie deep in the minds of Americans. Change requires the American public to admit to the truths that the coronavirus has forced us to face and the moral integrity to take action. Real change will require more than cosmetics, more than feel-good measures; it will take courage: unlearning more than three hundredyears of indoctrination will be difficult and uncomfortable. The journey to change imposed by the COVID-19 pandemic requires collective and individual effort; thus, the chapter "A Primer for Enlightened Whiteness" is a key aspect of this book.

The coronavirus has created awareness of racial and class divisions in American society. The damage of social inequality, fueled by an ideology of separation, division, individualism may be near impossible to repair. As a result, brewing racial division and class conflict will be detrimental to our nation's future. We have reached a choice point. At this critical juncture in our history, our nation's future depends on change. We must ask ourselves individually and as a nation, "Do we wish to persist as a nation being controlled by an ideology that promotes racism and classism or will we become the nation of our highest ideals? Do we as individuals and as a collective have the courage and the moral integrity to change?"

REQUIREMENTS OF CHANGE

For American society (individual and collective level) to change, the following acknowledgments, recognitions, and actions are essential:

- acknowledgment of the contradictions between America's stated ideals and the reality of life for many of its citizens;
- acknowledgment of the "invention" and intentional omissions rather than the true telling of American history;
- acknowledgment that a class system does exist in American society;

- acknowledgment of the hypocrisy related to the concept of "all" the people and the reality of life for persons of color and whites in lower socioeconomic classes in America;
- acknowledgment, confrontation, and challenge of the myths of white superiority and black inferiority as a key to change in the collective American mind;
- recognition of the creation and purpose of the social construction of "whiteness" and "blackness" as social control;
- recognition of the price paid by whites for the psychological cost of whiteness;
- recognition of the indoctrination of the inferiority of blackness on the policies and practices of American institutions of religion, healthcare, education, law enforcement, and finances;
- recognition that systematic racism continues to exist in American society despite the gains in civil rights and improvements that have occurred;
- recognition of the crucial relationship between racism and classism in American society;
- recognition of the use of racism to preserve the American class system;
- recognition of how the beliefs, values, and norms that underlie white supremacy ideology harm all Americans, white and those of color;
- recognition of how the dehumanization of those perceived to be the "other" through lack of human empathy, compassion, and moral integrity dehumanizes the white self;
- recognition of how individualism prevents class consciousness and collective action to resolve the suffering of those experiencing both racism and classism;
- recognition of how white supremacy ideology and the racism it promotes has shaped resentment and denigration of the poor in America;
- willingness to acknowledge, confront, and challenge the myths of white superiority and black inferiority that are key to preserving white supremacy ideology;
- willingness to refute the mythology of white supremacy ideology;
- willingness to engage in a critical analysis of American laws, policies, practices, and contradictions related to the ideals expressed in the Declaration of Independence and the Bill of Rights;
- willingness to establish a new definition of patriotism—respect and love enough for America to see it change for the better; to live up to its ideals;
- willingness to become part of a multiracial coalition to advocate for the economic and social equality of all Americans;

- willingness to develop a counter-narrative based on true American history taught at all levels of the educational system;
- willingness to no longer program generations of American children to believe in separateness, division, and the "other";
- commitment to tell future generations of children the truth of who they are and who they can become; and
- willingness to develop the courage to envision a new America built on its touted ideals.

VISION FOR A NEW AMERICA

This is the time for change; the time to envision a new America, a new American culture based on the principles defined in the Declaration of Independence and the Bill of Rights. The new American culture must come from "we the people." When those designated and perceived to be white no longer depend upon "whiteness" for a sense of identity, esteem, and selfhood, only then can class alliances and social equality for all occur.

Academic research, mainstream literature, and the investigations of the press have focused on the concept of "white privilege." However, the crucial elements of how racism is maintained and reinforced have not been addressed. The core element, the most insidious element related to white supremacy ideology and racism, lies in the indoctrination of the white mind. The lengthy generational propaganda designed for this purpose has been successful. As a result, many whites, especially those in the blind, perverse, and toxic state of whiteness, are holders and preservers of stereotypical images and language related to inferiority of blacks and superiority of whites.

Most critically, whiteness and the inherent racism attached prevent association, establishment of relationships, and alliances between common whites and blacks. Racism was and is still crucial to maintaining power by the ruling class. If the ruling class can keep whites and blacks from associating and forming alliances, then the two groups in their separateness have less power. They have less incentive to fix each other's plight, the same plight, which includes for both of them lack of: decent education, a living wage, decent housing, affordable healthcare, and decent treatment in general.

As we exit the second decade of the twenty-first century, there is an irrational fear of the loss of white status. It is stoked daily by some of the media and many politicians. The belief that whites have to remain atop other ethnic groups in the United States social hierarchy is deeply ingrained in the collective white mind. Whiteness provides a mythical deserved place at the top of the racial hierarchy and promotes a fierce investment in a sense of whiteness that has nothing to do with freedom for all. It is the myth of black inferiority that supports the sense of white superiority. Racism in the United States is dependent on the persistent reinforcement of the myth of black inferiority. Until it is no longer expedient for the media and political figures to exploit the myth of black inferiority, the myth of white superiority will endure. Neither whites nor the country as a whole benefit from the ideology of white supremacy. A divisiveness of this magnitude harms every single one of us and the very fabric of our democracy.

"Whiteness" must be addressed because its mythology enables racism to flourish in American society. Whiteness is a social construction and a tool for controlling the majority white population. According to historian David Roediger (1994), "Whiteness is a destructive ideology that must be exposed, demystified, and demeaned, rather than focusing on the social construction of race generally." Roediger says that the rejection of whiteness is part of the process that both attacks racism and allows a sense of recovery from oppression by white workers. In attacking racism, "If it does not involve a critique of whiteness, the questioning of racism often becomes shallow and limited."

CONCLUSION

The message of this book is that "whiteness" and the racism it produces hurts all Americans, whites as well as blacks. Knowing the history of whiteness and the ways in which the stereotypical images of blacks were used to maintain an image of white superiority provides answers to white identity anxiety and creates a route to psychological freedom to white Americans. The creation of racism in the United States cannot and will not be resolved until white Americans are free from believing in a mythology called whiteness.

Classism is real in American life; it is critical that middle and working-class whites understand how class status makes for a need for attachment to whiteness. Addressing the relationship between classism and racism requires strict attention, just as the making of second-class citizens out of blacks and poor whites was repeated until it became believed. Until the two critical factors that maintain racism in the nation—until the concept of whiteness and its relationship to classism have been addressed—the racial sphere in America will be unchanged.

We, all of us, will continue to be oppressed by the destructive white supremacy culture. White supremacy ideology has been used for generations to divide and ultimately control all Americans. The racism practiced has come at the expense of any long-term welfare of our nation.

This book is written for white Americans who have sustained more than three hundred years of indoctrination that has controlled their beliefs, attitudes, assumptions, perceptions, and actions related to blacks and other people of color. Wellness requires whites to give up the psychological safety, their material and symbolic standing of whiteness; wellness requires refuting the mythology of whiteness. The intention of this book, written with empathy and compassion for blacks and whites — and the fervent hope of this book — is to begin the process of white liberation in our nation. Only this will lead to racial healing. This is the moment, the time for change.

Afterword

In contemplating what to write in this afterword, I happened upon the movie *IO*, in which the character played by Anthony Mackie quoted from Plato's *Symposium*: "So ancient is the desire for one another which is implanted in us. Reuniting our original nature, seeking to make one of two and healing the state of man."

After which, he proceeded to explain the meaning of this quote. He said: "Each of us, when separated, is always looking for our other half. It's our nature. But when one is met with this other half . . . the pair are lost in an amazement of love, friendship, intimacy. And one will not be seen out of the other's sight. See, the reason is, human nature was once originally one. And we were whole. And the desire and the pursuit of the whole . . . is called love."

This soliloquy provides a very succinct description of our highest ideal as Americans. It is human nature to connect with each other deeply, to empathize with each other, to anticipate each other's needs, and to create the conditions that support the full expression of every individual's full creative potential. Humanness is the constant process of living based on the model of that which created us, which is unity: loving one's neighbor as one's self.

We have allowed ourselves to be taken off the higher path where we live in the pursuit of becoming the very best versions of ourselves, and instead have taken the lesser road based on comparison with others rather than self-cultivation. For too long we have been distracted from our true purpose, which is to be the best human beings possible. This purpose is what the education of our children must be based on; and how we create public policy.

The success of our country depends on each person contributing their God-given gifts and talents to the betterment of our society. It is our job in life to discover our gifts and to assist others in the discovery of theirs. This is what it is to be a human being.

When we allow ourselves to be lulled into accepting the expectation of advantage, as a substitute for applying oneself fully to every opportunity afforded to us, it creates a unique paradox. In waiting for advantage based on an assumed social hierarchy, we miss the opportunities provided to us to improve our lives through self-cultivation, whereas these same opportunities are capitalized on by the very persons whom we feel superior to. Despite the hardships they endure, they advance in society based on their tenacity in regard to appreciating and taking advantage of the smallest of opportunities availed to them.

This paradox is one that has played out between our country's social majorities and minorities, and with its immigrant communities. We have been more concerned with maintaining contrived social hierarchies rather than using every moment as an opportunity to become the best version of ourselves and achieve our full potential as individuals and as a nation.

We have allowed our country's productive capacity to deteriorate to the point where we are now more consumers than producers. The only way in which our citizens will be able to live at the highest quality of life, henceforth, is for us to restore our productive capacity as a nation, which requires the utilization of the skills and talents of every American.

We cannot neglect any child, any neighborhood, any community. No one can be left behind. We are at a point in which, either the combined human greatness of our society will be fully revealed and we will achieve unimagined creative heights for our society, or our national creative potential will continue to lie in a resting state, in which we will lose our competitive advantage as a country and our national quality of life will degrade. It is in this state of full expression of our humanity that we will once again fall in love with each other. And, when this happens, we can never be separated again.

Jaha F. Cummings

Appendix A–G

Virus: an infectious agent that replicates inside the living cells of a host; from the Latin word meaning slimy liquid or poison.

Biological Virus	Sociological Virus
Virus particles attach to the host cell.	The collective American mind becomes the host cell for the virus of white supremacy ideology.
After penetration, the invading virus releases its genetic instruction into the host cells.	Using racist demagoguery and propaganda, the American mind becomes infected with racism.
The viral infection causes dramatic ideology structural changes in the host cell; producing a number of diseases, e.g., small pox, Ebola, etc.	The virus of white supremacy produces the disease of racism.
Damage to the cells makes it impossible for the organism to function normally.	The virus of white supremacy makes it impossible for America to function as a free equal society.
Viruses leave their traces on the history of life.	The virus of white supremacy has infected the collective American mind for four hundred years.

APPENDIX B: MISCEGENATION LAWS

Twenty-five states ultimately enacted anti-miscegenation laws; the first laws that criminalized love, sexual intimacy, and marriage between whites and non-whites occurred during the Colonial Era. Rather than class, or enslaved status, race became the basis for restricting one's choice of a marriage partner. By 1776, twelve of the thirteen colonies outlawed Afro-European intermarriage and passing (the acceptance of a mixed-race individual as being white).

In the collective American mind, the separation of the races under intimate conditions was normal and natural. Also, most Americans only saw these laws as punitive measures toward blacks, especially black men. However, from the anti-miscegenation laws cited below, one can see that

68   *Appendix A–G*

these laws were directed to control the human emotions and choices of whites as well.

- 1705: The Massachusetts colonial legislature passes law prohibiting marriage and fornication between negroes or mulattoes and whites. In 1786, the ban on fornication was removed, but the ban on mixed marriages was expanded to include Indians. (Massachusetts)
- Intermarriage: The marriage of a person of Caucasian blood with a Negro, Mongolian, Malay, or Hindu shall be null and void. (Arizona)
- Intermarriage: All marriages between a white person and a negro, or between a white person and a person of negro descent to the fourth generation inclusive, are hereby forever prohibited. (Florida)
- Intermarriage: It shall be unlawful for a white person to marry anyone except a white person. Any marriage in violation of this section shall be void. (Georgia)
- Intermarriage: All marriages between a white person and a negro, or between a white person and a person of negro descent, to the third generation, inclusive, or between a white person and a member of the Malay race; or between the negro and a member of the Malay race; or between a person of Negro descent, to the third generation, inclusive, and a member of the Malay race, are forever prohibited, and shall be void. (Maryland)
- Intermarriage: The marriage of a white person with a negro or mulatto or person who shall have one-eighth or more of negro blood, shall be unlawful and void. (Mississippi)
- Intermarriage: All marriages between . . . white persons and negroes or white persons and Mongolians . . . are prohibited and declared absolutely void. . . . No person having one-eighth part or more of negro blood shall be permitted to marry any white person, nor shall any white person be permitted to marry any negro or person having one-eighth part or more of negro blood. (Missouri)
- Intermarriage: All marriages of white persons with Negroes, Mulattos, Mongolians, or hereafter contracted in the State of Wyoming are and shall be illegal and void. (Wyoming)

A second set of anti-miscegenation laws were enacted during the 1860s.

- 1863: Anti-miscegenation law included in the state constitution. (West Virginia)
- 1864: Miscegenation [Statute] Marriages between whites with "Negroes, Indians, Mongolians" were declared illegal and void. The word "Descendants" does not appear in the statute. (Arizona)
- 1864: Miscegenation [Statute] Marriage between Negroes and mulattoes, and white persons "absolutely void." Penalty: Fine between

$50 and $550, or imprisonment between three months and two years, or both. (Colorado)

- 1865: Miscegenation [Statute] Declared marriage between whites and a Negro or mulatto as illegal. Penalty: Misdemeanor, with a fine up to $100, or imprisonment in the county jail up to six months, or both. (Nebraska)
- 1912: The state's miscegenation law offered an extensive list of inappropriate marriage candidates by race and color for Caucasians, including blacks, "Malay or brown race, Mongolian or yellow race, or Indian or red race." (Nevada)
- 1866: Miscegenation [Statute] Prohibited marriage between white persons and Negroes, Indians, or a person of half or more Negro or Indian blood. (Washington)
- 1866: This law prohibited whites from marrying any African American who is more than 12 percent African American (meaning having a blood relation up to the third generation to an African American). Penalty of not following this law was a felony that was punishable by imprisonment in the state penitentiary up to five years. (Kentucky)
- 1867: Miscegenation [Statute] Unlawful for any white person to intermarry with any "Negro, Chinese, or any person having one-quarter or more Negro, Chinese or kanaka blood, or any person having more than one-half Indian blood." Penalty: Imprisonment in the penitentiary or the county jail for between three months and one year. Those who licensed or performed such a ceremony could be jailed for three months to one year, or fined between $100 and $1,000.
- Enacted seven Jim Crow laws in the areas of education and miscegenation between 1869 and 1952: Persons who violated the miscegenation law could be imprisoned between one and ten years. (Indiana)
- 1870: Miscegenation [Constitution] Intermarriage prohibited between white persons and Negroes, or descendants of Negro ancestors to the third generation. (Tennessee)
- 1870: Miscegenation [Statute] Penalty for intermarriage between whites and blacks was labeled a felony, punishable by imprisonment in the penitentiary from one to five years. (Tennessee)
- 1872: Miscegenation [State Code] Prohibited intermarriage. Penalty: $1,000 fine, or up to six months' imprisonment. (Rhode Island)
- 1877: Miscegenation [Statute] Unlawful for a person of "pure white blood, who intermarries, or has illicit carnal intercourse, with any Negro or person having a distinct and visible admixture of African blood." Penalty: Fined up to $100, or imprisoned up to three months, or both. Any person who knowingly officiates such a mar-

riage charged with misdemeanor and fined up to $100 or imprisoned in three months, or both. (Ohio)

- 1888: Miscegenation [Chapter XLV, Laws of Utah, 1888.] Intermarriage prohibit between a Negro and a white person, and between a "Mongolian" and a white person. (Utah)

Anti-miscegenation laws were dehumanizing especially for whites as the myth of white superiority prevented them from pursuing and having normal interaction and relationships with other human beings other than whites. Jim Crow laws designed specifically to prevent social mixing of whites and blacks in the collective American mind as affecting only blacks, but again deny whites the right to socialize and establish human relationships of their choosing.

APPENDIX C

Following are the laws cited in *Black Laws of Virginia: A Summary of the Legislative Acts of Virginia Concerning Negroes from the Earliest Times to the Present* pertaining to free blacks:

- 1670. Act V. Negroes or Indians, though baptized and enjoying their own freedom, shall be incapable of purchasing Christians, yet they are not deterred from buying any of their own nation.
- 1691. Act XVI. Negroes who are free must be transported out of the country by the person freeing them freedom within six months after such setting free.
- 1705. Chapter XLIX. No Negro, although Christian, shall purchase any Christian servant, except his own complexion, or such as are declared slaves. If any Negro shall purchase any Christian white servant, the servant shall become free.
- 1723. Chapter IV. No Negro or Indian slave shall be set free upon any pretense whatsoever, except for some meritorious service adjudged by the governor.
- 1793. Chapter 22. Free Negroes or mulattoes shall be registered and numbered in a book to be kept by the town clerk, which shall specify age, name, color, status and by whom, and in what court emancipated.
- 1793. Chapter 23. This act forbids free Negroes or mulattoes from migrating into the Commonwealth. If they come in, they may be exported to the place from which they came. Every master of a vessel or other person who shall bring into this Commonwealth by water or by land any free Negro shall forfeit one hundred pounds, one-half to the Commonwealth and the other half to the informer.
- 1806. Chapter 94. A free Negro is not to carry any firelock of any kind without a license. For a second offense he shall in addition to

forfeiting all such arms be punished with stripes, at the discretion of the justice not exceeding thirty-nine.

- 1831. Chapter XXXIX. Free Negroes and mulattoes who remain in the Commonwealth contrary to law are to be sold publicly. After the Nat Turner insurrection, laws regarding both free Negroes and enslave became more restrictive.

APPENDIX D: IRISH AND AFRICAN AMERICAN STEREOTYPICAL IMAGES

Irish	African American
Ape-like features/appearance	Ape-like features/appearance
Wild Beast	Brute
Thomas Nash cartoon of Irishman lighting a powder keg and swinging a whiskey bottle.	The Italian propaganda poster: How black American GIs handle art. A black GI as a Brute with the *Venus de Milo*.
Language	
Inferior race	Inferior race
Uncivilized	Uncivilized
Violent	Violent
Criminal	Criminal
Rapist	Rapist
Lazy	Lazy
Barbarous	Barbarous
Ignorant	Ignorant
Superstitious	Superstitious
Filthy Sexual Habits	Overly sexual
Laws	
No systematic racial subordination by laws	Jim Crow Laws

APPENDIX E: THE ROLE OF IMAGES AND LANGUAGE IN DEHUMANIZING BLACKS

Image	Language	Desired Emotional Response
Sambo		
Exaggerated physical features; head bowed; subservient posture; grinning	Childlike; happy, content; loyal	Comfort; security; positive feelings about the humanness and moral right of slavery
Dandy		
"Putting on airs"	Doesn't know his place; buffoon	Anger, repugnancy
Shiftless/lazy		
Poorly dressed, shooting craps; eating watermelon, chicken stealing; hangover	Irresponsible; good for nothing	Disgust; repugnancy
Brute		
Animal-like in appearance; monstrous beast; crazed with lust	Savage, dangerous; demon; destructive; violent; criminal; rapist	Fear; enraged anger; need to punish and control
Mammy		
Dark skinned; obese, oversized lips and large teeth; head rag covering hair. Contentment satisfaction with role; hearty laugh	Loyal; faithful servant	Safety; maternal figure
Jezebel		
Naked; scantily dressed; seductive; beguiling; alluring	Hypersexual; lewd; worldly; loose morals	Disgust, contempt, rationalization of rape of black women

APPENDIX F

The American culture has been defined by the stereotypical images of blacks. The role of these stereotypical images in shaping American culture cannot be underestimated. Throughout the history of the nation from the colonial days until the twenty-first century, these images have influenced the beliefs, assumptions, perceptions, attitudes, and feelings of white Americans. There is barely an element of American culture that has been untouched by white supremacy ideology and the stereotypical images of African Americans used to preserve it. Aspects of observable or surface culture with stereotypical images of blacks include:

- Food: images of blacks eating watermelon or fried chicken.
- Arts: from minstrel shows which portrayed blacks as ignorant, buffoonish, and superstitious to *The Birth of a Nation* featuring the black Brute to *Gone with the Wind*, the stereotypical black prevailed.
- Music/lyrics: "Coon" songs, for example, Looney Coons Cakewalk and Two-step were popular aspects of American culture.
- Popular culture: games, notions, cartoons, and postcards featuring blacks as "alligator bait" were used to instill the white supremacy ideology in the American culture. Children's books, that is, *Gold Dust Twins* comic books, *Little Black Sambo*, to "Eenie meenie, miny moe, catch a n----- by his toe" had as their basis the stereotypical image of the black.
- Heroes/monuments/flags/regional holidays: memorialize and revere those that represent and glorify periods of history that exemplify white superiority and black inferiority.

The repetition and reinforcement of white supremacy ideology is deeply embedded in almost all aspects of American culture. These elements of white supremacy ideology remain in American culture in the twenty-first century.

APPENDIX G

Blind Whiteness	Perverse Whiteness	Toxic Whiteness	Enlightened Whiteness
Whiteness is natural; the normal state of affairs	Use whiteness to meet racially conditioned needs, i.e., esteem, personal power	Deep-seated belief in white supremacy and superiority	Human vs. "whiteness" focus
Complacency; acts of racial violence are justified and normal	Deceit—a primary characteristic	Psychopathic racial anger expressed in racial violence	Engages in self-reflection
Selfhood defined strictly in terms of whiteness	Use of institutional power to engage in racist actions	Obsessive need to preserve white supremacy	Openness to growth; pursues accurate knowledge related to race/racism

Unable to see relationship between racism and classism	Deliberate and immoral acts to harm blacks	Intense anger and resentment toward black progress, political, educational, and economic	Critical analysis of relationship between racism and classism
Does not critically analyze assumptions about whiteness and stereotypes of blacks and other people of color	Racial hoaxes—typical	Engages in subhuman acts of violence	Empathy and compassion
Conforms to rules of white superiority	Promotion of stereotypical images to gain desired results	Uses racial stereotypes, demagoguery to incite racial violence	Resists white supremacy ideology
		Promotes racist practices and policies	
		Ostracizes, punishes, even murders those who violate the rules of white supremacy	

APPENDIX H: ENLIGHTENED WHITENESS

A Conversation

PeggyDawn, Robert Moran, Colleen (observer), and I (Martha Bireda) sat down for our conversation on a sunny afternoon in the attractive, welcoming home the Morans had recently purchased in a quiet over-fifty-five community. They had recently moved from a larger home in an upscale canal community. Both PeggyDawn and Robert were chosen for this conversation because of their irreproachable honesty. (Please see their bios.)

MB: Thank you so much for agreeing to have this conversation with me. I believe you have much to offer others, perhaps those struggling with the issue of class and race.

PDM/RM: Thank you for inviting us. We are happy to be involved and to help in any way that we can.

RM: I have a black son-in-law and am very aware of the issues.

MB: So, let's get started. PeggyDawn, you are very open and forth-coming about growing up, as you describe it, as a "poor white coal miner's daughter." When and how did you first become aware of your class status?

PDM: I must have been ten or eleven years old when I met the older daughter of my boss. She didn't look like us [poor whites], her cloth-ing, hair, everything about her was different from us. Her dress had been purchased, it fit her body; we wore the boxy clothes that my mother sewed. Even her hair, she had long hair, ours was always cut short, I guess because it was easier to care for short hair. She was pretty and very classy. She had a "special," richer feel about her; she had access to better clothes, a better diet. She was the kind of woman who could get her way.

MB: So, what messages did you get about your place in the social class ladder?

PDM: That day, I wanted to speak to, connect with the rich girl, but my mother was furious. She said to me, "Keep your place" and "Know your place." My place was poor white trash.

RM: While I grew up in a small mining town in West Virginia, I was not considered a poor white. I grew up living a "white privileged" life. My father owned a print shop and was well known around town. My place in the social order was very different from PeggyDawn's.

MB: PeggyDawn, you have talked about the hopelessness that was part of being a poor white, especially the impact upon your father and other relatives. Tell me about that.

PDM: I admired and respected my father but he was depressed. He felt like a grunt in the mine, below a human. He talked about being underground all of the time. For forty years, we wept. My mother, Dorothy, sewed bras and was allowed to drive. Finally, Dorothy told my father Sam we were moving to Cleveland. This was a stepping stone for us. Among my sisters, however, there was a sense of hope-lessness; they connected with abusive men, drank, and didn't try for a better life.

MB: When and how did you avoid succumbing to the hopelessness and shame felt by some poor whites?

PDM: Early on I made the decision not to be poor and hopeless. I wanted to be Andrea Mitchell, the news journalist. I wanted to go to Pennsylvania State, but was discouraged by my family because I was not a male. My family needed me to work. I did, however, listen to the radio to learn standard English.

MB: Yes, I notice that you do not have a mountain accent. (We both laugh.) So how was your life in Cleveland?

PDM: I learned to live graciously without money or with very little money. I did feel inferior because I did not have a college degree. After I married, we were doing well enough to move to Shaker Heights. The people who lived there had been wealthy all of their lives. They never had to struggle for money or status. I felt different, felt inferior.

MB: (Turning to Robert) We haven't heard very much from you. What are your thoughts about the construct of whiteness?

RM: There is really no benefit to whiteness. It paralyzes our brain, keeps you closed-minded, unable to accept anything new or different. It's irrationality; the need to feel superior to somebody.

MB: Then why do you believe whites attach to the construct?

RM: It meets their psychological need. There is the fear of being displaced; that those from South of the Border will have more rights and power than whites.

MB: I have noticed a willingness of middle- and upper-class whites to help poor black children but not poor white children; what is this about?

RM: Shame; racism equals a shame base. There is more judgment of the poor white child, brings down the race. Want nothing to do with poor whites because it can be a reminder that we [whites] came from that. Can be a white savior to blacks. Why are whites like that? Some family shame. In my own family, my mother constantly warned us about class. Learned much later that there was some family shame of which she needed to hide.

MB: So, have there been any instances where you have had to examine your beliefs and feelings about race and racism?

PDM: When I was in my twenties, I saw how blacks were treated, but I disassociated [self-defense mechanism], said it had nothing to do with me. When times became really hard for me, I would say "at least I'm not black," but not in the way that I felt superior but understanding how much worse blacks were treated.

RM: Growing up there was only one black family in my town. The word went around to watch out for blacks, but my father was probably more prejudiced toward Italians. He wanted me to go to the "American" barber and not the Italian barber. My son-in-law is black, he is a wonderful husband to my daughter and from him I have gained so much.

MRB: Thank you so much for your time, and of course your openness and honesty.

BIOS: PEGGYDAWN AND ROBERT MORAN

PeggyDawn Moran; born December 30, 1936; hometown—St. Michael, Pennsylvania

A small coal mining town eighty miles east of Pittsburgh. The town built up after the South Fork dam broke and flooded Johnstown. Over two thousand people died and the wealthiest men in the world lost their playground. By the time I was born the summer homes and mansions were like ghosts haunting the town of St. Michael. The buildings nestled in amidst the small company houses built by the mining company to house the miner's families, including me. This emblem and constant reminder of disparity of wealth and the legends heard over and over of how the industrialists neglected the dam and refused to pay reparations, formed a lifetime struggle with prejudice toward the ultra-rich in me.

I have one brother. We were poor white trash. I was named after a burlesque queen who my seventeen-year-old mother was reading about while pregnant. To her, a poorer-than-dirt coal miner's daughter and wife, it seemed an upwardly mobile aspiration. I learned to love my name in later years, but hated it for a while in my teens.

I didn't know anything about black people. After moving to Cleveland, Ohio, following graduation from high school, I took the rapid transit to downtown Cleveland to shop at Higbee's. Often, while traveling through Cleveland's ghetto in the late fifties, into the sixties, I saw race rioting going on and thought, "those poor people." That's all. I accepted the situation as "part of life's cruel reality"—like miners who were considered less than human by the upper classes.

I met a wonderful black woman while working at GE in the late sixties and we became close friends. She was my maid of honor in my second marriage. She introduced me to people who made me wish I had grown up black. They were able to have fun. They loved to sing and dance. I envied their spirituality and joie de vivre.

I have two children and two grandchildren.

I've become an activist for racial justice and believe strongly that we are all one race.

Robert L. Moran; born in 1941, a win; hometown—Shinnston, West Virginia

A small coal mining town in north central West Virginia. Population two thousand.

Father owned a Job Shop Printing Company and my twin brother, Ronald, and I worked there a few hours a week.

There was only one black kid in town. We played baseball sometimes. He went to Clarksburg for school. Our school was integrated in 1958.

My father was well known around town and we lived a "white privilege" life. He died when I was fourteen years old. My world was turned upside down. Mother had to move to Elyria, Ohio, for a teaching job. The print shop was sold for parts.

At sixteen I moved back to Shinnston on my own. Worked my way through junior year of high school working at Tetrick Funeral Home—helping at funerals, driving the hearse as an ambulance, and embalming.

After a year I moved back to Elyria with my family and graduated in 1959. Army for three years, then back to Ohio.

APPENDIX I: LETTER FROM ROBERT'S FRIEND DAVID

My good friend Dave: I met Dave about 1965 working at American Ship Building Company, located on the Black River in Lorain, Ohio.

We both left the ship building and started working as Boilermakers. The Boilermakers build pressure vessels, it's hard, dirty, and dangerous work.

We became good friends. Working together many times during the over thirty years, at times depending on another to do these dangerous jobs. That in itself brings men together.

After retiring we both took up sailing. Doing open ocean racing and sailing for fun. I was visiting Dave about three years ago, and as I was leaving, we were walking up the drive discussing social problems when he told me this story.

Dave's father owned a one-man auto repair garage in Williamsburg, Pennsylvania. He catered to both blacks and whites in this small community. One night in 1949 he was walking to a bar to meet a friend. He was jumped from behind by a black man and stabbed several times in the back.

Puncturing one lung and kidney. Some men in town got him to a hospital. His life was saved. Right after he was stabbed, the attacker pulled Dave's father's shoulder up, looked at him, and said, "Damn, I got the wrong man."

After a long recovery he reopened his auto repair garage. He noticed that his nine-year-old son was no longer friendly to his black friends.

Dave's father took Dave to the local black beer joint one evening. The black men in the bar cheered as he walked in the bar. He had many well-wishers as he downed several beers. Dad says to Dave, "These people are my friends, I notice that you are holding some bad thoughts of my friends. Don't let your judgment of one man be the judgment of all."

This story rocked me to the core.

All the time I have been with Dave since 1965, working, sailing, and hanging out, he never mentioned this part of his life. I knew he was not prejudice against blacks or anyone and now I know Dave just a little more.

I have always considered Dave as a very good friend. Now I know another part of the reason why.

APPENDIX J: "THE HOLLER"

Are there spaces where humanity rather than race prevails?

"The Holler"

In the holler lived the Russells, my black family, and two white families, the Coleys and Kirkos. Sarah and Will Coley lived next door to my grandmother, Lelia Russell, and across the road from my Aunt Rosa and Uncle James. Mrs. Kirkos, a widow, lived across the road from my home.

We were in our way an interdependent, self-contained community, not so much defined by race, but by our being "country" rather than town dwellers. Each day the men, black and white, drove up the narrow winding road to the top of the hill. Around the dangerous, steep curve, lay the world of race. Up the hill and around the curve, my father Alonzo and Uncle James became black; Will, our neighbor, became white. Because I was so young, I didn't know what indignities they faced daily, but at the end of the day they returned to the safety of the holler.

Sarah and Will Coley, the newest residents, lived in the most modern house with a well, modern appliances, and a telephone; the telephone of which my grandmother, Lelia, and Aunt Rosa had liberal use. My grandmother Lelia lived in a white frame house with green trim on which there were two swings. One had to climb steps made from large stones to reach the porch. What I remember most about the house was the kitchen with the coal and wood-burning stove that spanned the length of the house. Outside were an outhouse and a large terraced garden that climbed the hill in back of the house.

My uncle James, or Jim, as he was called by blacks and whites, and my Aunt Rosa lived across the road in an unpainted, weathered house. Beside the house sat the outhouse, a small shack my uncle used as a "man cave," and smokehouse. Near the road sat the weathered barn filled with hay where the work horses and horses for show were kept.

A rock path took one down past the oval track, the center filled with tobacco plants, where horses were ridden and tamed, a pigsty to the creek, and the spring, which was the source of drinking water.

We lived in an old house originally built in the 1920s by my grand-uncle. The four-room house sat on a slope of land high above the creek. Beside the house was our garden and further away our outhouse. We lived across the road from Mrs. Kirko, who lived in a small house covered with tar paper shingles.

The folks in the holler exchanged meats and vegetables.

The Coleys had cows and my uncle pigs. At the top of the hill, in a very weathered house, lived a white, Roy Bee, and his family. He rented from and worked for my uncle in the holler. I am not sure this could have occurred around and atop the steep curve. The cardinal rule of blacks and whites eating and drinking together was broken every weekend. Whites gathered with my uncle and his brothers on that day to drink moonshine or bourbon underneath my uncle's house. They sat for hours drinking and telling jokes and lies.

Beyond the steep curve in town, blacks and whites were separated from each other by a wall in the Broad Street Tearoom, an establishment owned by Mr. Sharp, a black man. Blacks and whites could peer into each other's space, but could not legally drink together. In the holler those laws were broken.

As folks in the holler, blacks and whites climbed and rounded the steep curve, the specter of race entering their lives. The whites became "white" but not in the same way as those who lived in antebellum mansions along Highway 11 or in the solidly middle- and upper-class Wassona Park. My father and uncles became "colored" with all the conventions of Jim Crow.

I am sure that my father and uncles, as well as our white neighbors, breathed a sigh of relief when they rounded that steep curve that brought them home to the holler. There they became simply "human."

A Primer for Enlightened Whiteness

The "change" needed to create a new American culture based upon the ideals laid out in the Declaration of Independence begins with the individual. The racist propaganda inculcated in the collective American mind was designed to influence the beliefs, values, attitudes, and behavior of the individual.

This primer focuses on the "awareness" and "actions" engaged by the individual that will help to bring about the required change in American society. The awareness and action exercises are related to each chapter of *A Time for Change*.

The achievement of awareness comes through open, honest responses to the items and a willingness to grow, to develop the full human capacity for empathy and compassion. Courage and the will to be part of the solution are required to successfully complete the action segment of the Primer.

Take a deep breath and begin the exercises. Your commitment to being the change that you would like to see occur in American culture and society is the ultimate act of patriotism.

AWARENESS EXERCISES—CHAPTER 1

Remember: Answer honestly and openly. There is no blame, shame, or correct answer. We are all in this together, trying to find answers to a problem that none of us is responsible for its creation.

Racial Identity Exercise

1. How do you identify racially?

_____

_____

_____

_____

Messages

1. If you identify as white, what messages do you receive about whiteness?

_____

_____

From parents and family?

_____

_____

_____

From neighborhood?

_____

_____

_____

From peers?

_____

_____

_____

From school?

_____

_____

_____

_____

Identity

1. How important is race (whiteness) to your sense of self?

_____

_____

_____

2. In what ways have/do you organize your identity around race?

_____

_____

How consciously has/does race affect your choice of where to live, shop, or send your children to school?

_____

_____

_____

_____

Attitudes/Experiences

1. What are your basic fears relate to "race"?

_____

_____

_____

_____

2. What has been your experience(s) with those who did not identify as white?

_____

_____

_____

_____

3. How have your background or experiences contributed to your attitudes about race relations?

_____

_____

_____

_____

4. In what ways do your attitudes toward persons who do not identify as white differ from those of your parents? Family? Peers?

_____

_____

_____

_____

_____

_____

_____

Action Steps—Chapter 1

- Learn how you became "white." Refer to the recommended reading list.
- Disavow the ideology of white supremacy. Open your mind and learn about the brutality of racism.
- Commit to "change" rather than surrendering to white shame or guilt.

- Ask forgiveness from any person that you believe you have offended because of your attachment to whiteness.
- Begin a program of self-actualization. Develop your talents and abilities so that your esteem is not based upon the false identity of whiteness.
- Seek out mutually respectable relationships with people of color. Ask them to be allies in your journey toward liberation.

AWARENESS—CHAPTER 2

1. Ethnic group: Having to do with the country from which a particular group or its ancestors originated.
2. Cultural assimilation: The process which takes place when one ethnic group acquires the behavior, values, perspectives, and characteristics of another cultural group and sheds its own cultural characteristics.

Ethnic Identity Exercise:

1. From what country did your ancestors come to America? When?

_____
_____
_____
_____

2. My ethnic heritage (parents/ grandparents) is:

_____
_____
_____
_____

3. What are the dominant beliefs/values/customs of your ethnic/cultural group?

_____
_____
_____
_____

4. How was your ethnic/cultural group defined to you by your family and community when you were growing up?

_____
_____

5. What are positive aspects of belonging to your ethnic/cultural group?

6. What are negative aspects of belonging to your ethnic/cultural group?

7. Do you identify most with your racial designation or your ethnic/cultural group? Why so?

Why not?

8. When and how did your ethnic/cultural group become "white"?

9. Who are you without whiteness defining your identity, esteem, and sense of self?

10. How comfortable are you identifying yourself by your ethnic origin rather than the social construction of "whiteness"?

_____

_____

Action Steps—Chapter 2

- Reclaim your ethnic identity; for example, Scotch-Irish, Italian American, and so on.
- Have the courage to check "other" on official documents; write in your ethnic identity.
- If not connected, connect with an organization that promotes and celebrates your ancestral ethnic identity(ies).

AWARENESS—CHAPTER 3

1. When did you first learn the place of blacks in the social hierarchy of America? At what age? Under what circumstances?

_____
_____
_____
_____
_____
_____
_____

2. What stereotypes of blacks have you heard? At what age? Under what circumstances?

_____
_____
_____
_____
_____
_____
_____

3. Did you have black help in your home? Did this person have to be subservient to you as a child? Where do you believe your parents placed this person in the social hierarchy? Did they see this person as having any attributes other than that of being a servant?

_____
_____
_____

_____
_____
_____
_____

4. Did you have ethnic notions in your home as a child? What subliminal messages did these objects provide about the role of blacks in society?

_____
_____
_____
_____

5. What if any rules associated with how you were to relate to blacks did you learn? How and why were these rules explained to you?

_____
_____
_____
_____

6. What stereotypes of blacks are most difficult for you to release? Why so?

_____
_____
_____
_____

Action Steps — Chapter 3

Develop a plan/process to work on eliminating stereotypes that you find difficult to release.

1. _____

2. _____

3. _____

4. _____

5. _____

AWARENESS—CHAPTER 4

A myth is a story without a determinable basis of fact. Mythology consists of a body of myths.

1. With which myths have you been indoctrinated with reference to whiteness or blackness?

_____
_____
_____
_____
_____
_____
_____
_____

2. To which source do you attribute most of your indoctrination?

_____
_____
_____
_____
_____

3. How have you been shaped by the idea/construction of whiteness?

_____
_____
_____

4. With what fears have you been indoctrinated related to blackness? Black men in particular?

_____
_____
_____
_____

Action Steps—Chapter 4

- Acknowledge, confront, and challenge the beliefs you hold as a result of white supremacy indoctrination.

AWARENESS—CHAPTER 5

1. What state of "whiteness" defines who I am? Why so? (Think deeply, no blame or shame, simply honesty for one's growth.)

_____
_____
_____
_____
_____
_____
_____

2. What, if any, of the racially conditioned needs do I experience? In what ways do I experience/deal with these needs?

_____
_____
_____
_____
_____
_____
_____
_____
_____

3. Have I ever knowingly used "whiteness" to my advantage? If yes, how so?

_____
_____
_____
_____
_____
_____

Action Steps—Chapter 5

Set a goal and develop a plan of action to embrace and express "enlightened whiteness." My goal:

1. _____

2. _____

3. _____
   _____

4. _____

5. _____

AWARENESS—CHAPTER 6

1. To what social class did you belong as a child? How did your family define your class?

_____
_____
_____

2. Did you feel advantaged by your social class as a child? If so, what advantages did you enjoy?

_____
_____
_____

3. Have you ever felt like an outsider because of your social class? If so, when and how?

_____
_____
_____

4. Have you ever been discriminated against or disadvantaged because of your social class? If so, when and how?

_____
_____
_____

5. Have you ever felt that "whiteness" failed you? If so, when and how?

_____
_____
_____
_____
_____

6. Have you ever been condescending to those in a lower class than yours regardless of race? If so, how and when?

_____

_____

_____

_____

7. Have you ever used derogatory terms—for example, "pwt" (poor white trash), "hillbilly"—to describe whites in a lower social class than your own? If so, for what reasons/circumstances?

_____

_____

_____

_____

Action Steps—Chapter 6

- Acknowledge and address any issues of classism that you may have.
- Make a commitment to work for both racial and class equality.

AWARENESS—CHAPTER 7

1. Am I willing to release the illusory identity and consciousness of whiteness? If so, for what reason(s)? If not, for what reason(s)?

_____

_____

_____

2. As I examine Appendix H and I, what aspects of "enlightened whiteness" do these individuals demonstrate? Why so? Am I willing to change my consciousness to be more aligned with enlightened whiteness? If yes, why so? If not, why so?

_____

_____

_____

_____

_____

_____

_____

Action Steps — Chapter 7

Three crucial steps:

1. Decide to change: I am willing to see myself and others outside of the socially constructed labels of whiteness and blackness.
2. Decide to be changed: I am willing to let go of old beliefs based upon white supremacy ideology and develop a new mindset.
3. Decide to bring about change: I am willing to be an instrument of change, to help bring about racial and class healing through my actions and advocacy. I am ready to become a true American patriot by standing for and promoting the American ideals of freedom, justice, and opportunity for "all" Americans.

RECOMMENDED READING

1. *The Invention of the White Race: Volumes I and II* by Theodore Allen
2. *A People's History of the United States* by Howard Zinn
3. *Lies My Teacher Told Me* by James Loewen
4. *They Came Before Columbus* by Ivan Van Sertima
5. *Before the Mayflower: A History of the Negro in America, 1619–1962* by Lerone Bennett

GUIDELINES FOR EDUCATORS

Educators must be at the forefront of efforts to combat the destructive elements of white supremacy. The twenty-first century truly presents "the time for change"; the time to disrupt and refute the generational ideology that has produced racism in our society. Most crucial is a school district's establishment of a policy to combat white supremacy ideology through curricula change and professional development to use history as a tool to present a counternarrative to that based upon racist ideology. The bibliography in this book presents a starting point for references to develop a curriculum that presents a true history of the development of the nation. Below are suggestions for events and areas study in American history that are crucial to preventing the further indoctrination of American students with an ideology of racial mythology and hatred.

ERAS AND TOPICS TO EXPLORE IN AMERICAN HISTORY

The Colonial Era

- The use and treatment of indentured servants and enslaved Europeans in the establishment and development of the early colonies
- Status of Africans before creation of "whiteness"
- Bacon's Rebellion
- Runaways from the early colonies and the Dismal Swamp
- The creation of the concept of "whiteness"; why it was created, how it was reinforced and perpetuated
- Class differences and experiences among early settlers in the colonies

The Antebellum Era and Civil War

- The enslavement of Africans; how African enslavement produced a powerful economy for America; focus on the rice, cotton, and sugar industries in the nation
- The resistance of enslaved Africans; Maroon communities in the United States
- The state of poor white Americans during the enslavement era
- An analysis of the Civil War; southerners for and against secession and the reasons why

The Reconstruction/Post–Reconstruction Eras

- Gains for both white and black Americans during Reconstruction
- The return to white supremacy; who gained; methods used
- Racial terrorism in the United States; analysis of domestic versus foreign terrorism

The Jim Crow Era

- A thorough examination of the laws and customs
- The stereotypes created especially during this era that remain in the American collective consciousness
- Class consciousness: Why are there still poor whites after over a hundred years of blacks denied entrance to the American economy?

The Civil Rights Movement

- Explore activities and racial terrorism that occurred during the civil rights movement

- Critical analysis of the American creed and the denial of rights to African Americans
- White supremacist messages about rights of blacks and black leaders

Post–Civil Rights Movement

- The meaning of the election of President Barack Obama
- Present state of multi-racial relationships
- Immigration issues
- The importation of immigrants; the deportation of immigrants
- Immigration laws over time (reasons for changes)
- Present-day white supremacist views, messages, and activities related to non-whites, the Jewish and Muslim communities
- Creating a post–white-supremacist America

This is only a list of suggested topics; the list can be expanded to include events such as American expansion, the Mexican-American War, and the Indian Wars, in particular the Second Seminole War, or significant historical events in the state in which a school district is located.

Most critically, the curricula must help American students of all races, ethnicities, religions, to understand the origin and purpose for the creation of whiteness, the role of and impact of racism upon all Americans, the reality and influence of the American class system, and as future leaders, their crucial need to disavow the ideology and culture of white supremacy in American society.

Bibliography

Alderman, Clifford Lindsey. *Colonists for Sale: The Story of Indentured Servants in America*. New York: Macmillan Publishing Co. Inc., 1975.

Allen, Theodore W. *The Invention of the White Race, Volume II: The Origin of Racial Oppression in Anglo-America*. London: Verso, 1997.

Baldwin, James. *The Fire Next Time*. New York: Dell Publishing Co., Inc., 1963.

Ballagh, James Curtis. *White Servitude in the Colony of Virginia: A Study of the System of Indentured Labor in the American Colonies*. New York: Burt Franklin, 1969.

Battalora, Jacqueline. *Birth of a White Nation: The Invention of White People and Its Relevance Today*. Houston, TX: Strategic Book Publishing and Rights Co., 2013.

Bennett, H. S. *Life on the English Manor: A Study of Peasant Conditions 1150–1400*. Cambridge: Cambridge University Press, 1969.

Bennett, Lerone, Jr. *Before the Mayflower: The Negro in America*. New York: Penguin Books, 1970.

Bennett, Lerone, Jr. *The Shaping of Black America*. Chicago, IL: Johnson Publishing Company, 1975.

Bennett, Lerone, Jr. "The White Problem in America." In *White Racism: Its History, Pathology and Practice*, edited by Barry N. Schwartz and Robert Disch. New York: Dell Publishing Co., Inc., 1970.

Billings, David. *Deep Denial: The Persistence of White Supremacy in United States History and Life*. Rosell, NJ: Crandall, Dostie & Douglas Books, Inc., 2016.

Bireda, Martha. "The Mythical African American Male." *WEEA Digest*. Newton, MA: WEEA Resource Center, 2000.

Bolton, Charles C. *Poor Whites of the Antebellum South: Tenants and Laborers in Central North Carolina and Northeast Mississippi*. Durham, NC: Duke University Press, 1994.

Boskin, J. "Sambo: The National Jester in Popular Culture." In *The Great Fear*, edited by Gary Nash and Richard Weiss. New York: Holt, Rinehart & Winston, 1970.

Bowser, Benjamin P. and Hunt, Raymond G. (Eds.). *Impacts of Racism on White Americans*. Beverly Hills: Sage Publications, 1981.

Breen, T. H. *"Myne Owne Ground": Race and Freedom on Virginia's Eastern Shore, 1640–1676*. Oxford: Oxford University Press, 2004.

Brown, Gwen. *We Who Were Poor: Ending the Oppression of Classism*. Seattle, WA: Rational Island Publishers, 2000.

Burr, Sherri L. *Complicated Lives: Free Blacks in Virginia, 1619–1865*. Durham, NC: Carolina Academic Press, 2019.

Byrd, Herbert L., Jr. *Proclamation 1625: America's Enslavement of the Irish*. Victoria, BC: Friensen Press, 2016.

Callero, Peter L. *The Myth of Individualism: How Social Forces Shape Our Lives*. Lanham, MD: Rowman & Littlefield Publishers, 2009.

Coldam, Peter Wilson. *Emigrants in Chains: A Social History of Forced Emigration to the American Colonies of Felons, Destitute Children, Political and Religious Non-Conformists, Vagabonds, Beggars, and Other Undesirables 1607–1776*. Surrey, UK: Geneological Publishing Co., Inc., 1992.

Craven, Wesley Frank. *White, Red, and Black: The Seventeenth-Century Virginian*. Charlottesville: The University Press of Virginia, 1971.

Delaney, Arthur and Edwards-Levy, Ariel. "Americans Are Mistaken about Who Gets Welfare." *Huffpost*, February 5, 2018. https://www.huffpost.com/entry/americans-welfare-perceptions-survey_n_5a7880cde4b0d3df1d13f60b.

Delany, Lloyd T. "The White American Psyche Exploration of Racism." In *White Racism: Its History, Pathology and Practice*, edited by Barry N. Schwartz and Robert Disch. New York: Dell Publishing Co., Inc., 1970.

Dennis, Rutledge M. "Socialization and Racism: The White Experience." In *Impacts of Racism on White Americans*, edited by Benjamin P. Bowser and Raymond G. Hunt. Beverly Hills: Sage Publications, 1981.

Du Bois, W. E. B. *Black Reconstruction in America 1860–1880*. New York: The Free Press, 1998.

Dulles, Foster Rhea. *Labor in America: A History*. 3rd ed. New York: Thomas Y. Crowell Company, 1966.

DuRocher, Kristina. *Raising Racists: The Socialization of White Children in the Jim Crow South*. Lexington: The University Press of Kentucky, 2011.

Edsall, Thomas Byrne and Edsall, Mary D. *Chain Reaction: The Impact of Race, Rights and Taxes on American Politics*. New York: W.W. Norton & Company, 1991.

Ekirch, Roger A. *Bound for America: The Transportation of British Convicts to the Colonies, 1718–1775*. Oxford: Clarendon Press, 1987.

Entman, Robert M. and Rojecki, Andrew. *The Black Image in the White Mind: Media and Race in America*. Chicago: University of Chicago Press, 2001.

Fitzgerald, Michael W. *The Union League Movement in the Deep South: Politics and Agricultural Change During Reconstruction*. Baton Rouge: Louisiana State University Press, 1989.

Flynt, Wayne. *Dixie's Forgotten People: The South's Poor Whites*. Bloomington: Indiana University Press, 2004.

Franklin, John Hope. *From Slavery to Freedom*. 3rd ed. New York: Random House, 1967.

Gilens, Martin. *Why Americans Hate Welfare: Race, Media and the Politics of Antipoverty Policy*. Chicago: The University of Chicago Press, 1999.

Graham, Carol. *Happiness for All? Unequal Hopes and Lives in Pursuit of the American Dream*. Princeton, NJ: Princeton University Press, 2017.

Guild, June Purcell. *Black Laws of Virginia: A Summary of the Legislative Acts of Virginia Concerning Negroes from the Earliest Times to Present*. New York: Negro Universities Press, 2012.

Hacker, Andrew. *Two Nations*. New York: Macmillan, 1992.

Hadden, Sally E. *Slave Patrols: Law and Violence in Virginia and the Carolinas*. Cambridge, MA: Harvard University Press, 2001.

Hatch, Charles E. *The First Seventeen Years: Virginia 1607–1624*. Charlottesville: The University Press of Virginia, 1957.

Hayden, Harry. *The Story of the Wilmington Rebellion*. Wilmington: n.p., 1936.

Heatherton, Todd F., Kleck, Robert E., Hebl, Michelle R., Hull, Jay G. (Eds.). *The Social Psychology of Stigma*. New York: The Guilford Press, 2000.

Helper, Hinton. *The Impending Crisis of the South: How to Meet It*. New York: A.B. Burdick, 1860. First published in 1857.

Hoffman, Michael A. *They Were White and They Were Slaves: The Untold History of the Enslavement of Whites in Early America*. Coeur d' Alene, ID: The Independent History & Research Company, 1991.

Howell, Andrew J. *The Book of Wilmington*. Wilmington: Wilmington Publishing Company, 1930.

Hurwitz, Jon and Peffley, Mark. (Eds.). *Perception and Prejudice: Race and Politics in the United States*. New Haven: Yale University Press, 1998.

Jernegan, Marcus Wilson. *Laboring and Dependent Classes in Colonial America, 1607–1783*. New York: Frederich Ungar Publishing Co, 1931.

Johnston, James Hugo. *Race Relations in Virginia & Miscegenation in the South 1776–1860*. Amherst: University of Massachusetts Press, 1970.

Jordan, Don and Walsh, Michael. *White Cargo: The Forgotten History of Britain's White Slaves in America*. New York: New York University Press, 2007.

Karp, Joan B. "The Emotional Impact and a Model for Changing Racist Attitudes." In *Impacts of Racism on White Americans Beverly Hills*, edited by Benjamin P. Bowser and Raymond G. Hunt. Beverly Hills, CA: Sage Publications, 1981.

Katz, Phyllis A. (Ed.). *Towards the Elimination of Racism*. New York: Pergamom Press, Inc., 1976.

Liu, William Ming. *Social Class and Classism in the Helping Professions: Research, Theory, and Practice*. Los Angeles, CA: Sage, 2011.

Lockley, Timothy James. *Lines in the Sand: Race and Class in Lowcountry Georgia, 1750–1860*. Athens: The University of Georgia Press, 2001.

Lustig, Myron W. and Koester, Jolene. *Intercultural Competence: Interpersonal Communication Across Cultures*. 2nd ed. New York: Harper Collins-College Publishers, 1996.

McKay, Matthew and Fanning, Patrick. *Prisoners of Belief: Exposing & Changing Beliefs That Control Your Life*. Oakland, CA: New Harbinger Publications, 1991.

Merritt, Keri Leigh. *Masterless Men: Poor Whites and Slavery in the Antebellum South*. Cambridge: Cambridge University Press, 2017.

Metzl, Jonathan M. *Dying of Whiteness: How the Politics of Racial Resentment Is Killing America's Heartland*. New York: Basic Books, 2019.

Morgan, Edmund S. *American Slavery, American Freedom: The Ordeal of Colonial Virginia*. New York: W.W. Norton & Company, Inc., 1975.

Muhammad, Khalid Gibran. *The Condemnation of Blackness: Race, Crime and the Making of Modern Urban America*. Cambridge, MA: Harvard University Press, 2018.

Neeson, J. M. *Commoners: Common Rights, Enclosure and Social Change in England, 1700–1820*. Cambridge: Cambridge University Press, 1993.

Neuback, Kenneth J. and Cazenave, Noel A. *Welfare Racism: Playing the Race Card against America's Poor*. New York: Routledge, 2001.

Newby, I. A. *Jim Crow's Defense: Anti-Negro Thought in America 1900–1930*. Baton Rouge: Louisiana State University, 1965.

O'Callaghan, Sean. *To Hell or Barbados: The Ethnic Cleansing of Ireland*. Kerry, Ireland: Brandon, 2000.

Ordway, John A. "Some Emotional Consequences of Racism for Whites." In *Racism and Mental Health*, edited by Charles Willie et al. Pittsburgh: University of Pittsburgh Press, 1973.

Parent, Anthony S. *The Formation of a Slave Society in Virginia, 1660–1740*. Chapel Hill: University of North Carolina Press, 2003.

Pettigrew, Thom. "Racism and the Mental Health of White Americans: A Social Psychological View." In *Racism and Mental Health*, edited by Charles Willie et al. Pittsburgh, PA: University of Pittsburgh Press, 1973.

Pieterse, Jan Nederveen. *White on Black: Images of Africa and Blacks in Western Popular Culture*. New Haven: Yale University Press, 1995.

Pilgrim, David. *Understanding Jim Crow: Using Racist Memorabilia to Teach Tolerance and Promote Social Justice*. Oakland, CA: Ferris State University and PM Press, 2015.

Reich, Michael. *Racial Inequality: A Political Economic Analysis*. Princeton, NJ: Princeton University Press, 1981.

Roediger, David R. *How Race Survived US History: From Settlement to the Obama Phenomenon*. London: Vers, 2008.

Roediger, David R. *Toward the Abolition of Whiteness: Essays on Race, Politics and Working Class History*. London: Verso, 1994.

Rose, Willie Lee. *A Documentary History of Slavery in North America*. London: Oxford University Press, 1976.

Russell, John H. *The Free Negro in Virginia: 1619–1865*. New York: Dover Publications, Inc., 1965.

Russell, Katheryn K. *The Color of Crime: Racial Hoaxes, White Fear, Black Protectionism, Police Harassment, and Other Macroaggressions*. New York: New York University Press, 1998.

Schwartz, Barry N. and Disch, Robert. *White Racism: Its History, Pathology and Practice*. New York: Dell Publishing, 1970.

Schwarz, John E. and Volgy, Thomas J. *The Forgotten Americans*. New York: W.W. Norton & Company, 1992.

Sennett, Richard and Cobb, Jonathan. *The Hidden Injuries of Class*. New York: W.W. Norton, 1972.

Smith, Lillian. *Killers of the Dream*. New York: Norton, 1961.

Smith, Lillian. "The Mob and the Ghost." In *White Racism: Its History, Pathology and Practice*, edited by Barry N. Schwartz and Robert Disch. New York: Dell Publishing, Co. Inc., 1970.

Stanard, Mary Newton. *The Story of Bacon's Rebellion*. New York: The Neal Publishing Company, 1907.

Sweet, Frank W. *The Virginia Origin of the Two-Caste System*. Palm Coast, FL: Backintyme, 2000.

Thandeka. *Learning to be White: Money, Race and God in America*. New York: Continuum, 2000.

Williams, David. *Rich Man's War: Class, Caste, and Confederate Defeat in the Lower Chattahoochee Valley*. Athens: University of Georgia Press, 1998.

Williams, Joan C. *White Working Class: Overcoming Class Cluelessness in America*. Boston, MA: Harvard Business Review Press, 2017.

Willie, Charles V., Kramer, Bernard M. and Brown, Bertram S. (Eds). *Racism and Mental Health*. Pittsburgh, PA: University of Pittsburgh Press, 1973.

Winn, Denise. *The Manipulated Mind: Brainwashing, Conditioning and Indoctrination*. Cambridge, MA: Malor Books, 2000.

Wray, Matt. *Not Quite White: White Trash and the Boundaries of Whiteness*. Durham, NC: Duke University Press, 2001.

Wright, Bobby E. *The Psychopathic Racial Personality*. Chicago: Third World Press, 1984.

Zinn, Howard. *A People's History of the United States, 1492–Present*. New York: HarperCollins Publishers, 1999.

Zweig, Michael. *The Working Class Majority: America's Best Kept Secret*. Ithaca: Cornell University Press, 2000.

About the Author

Martha R. Bireda, PhD, is director of the Blanchard House Museum of African American History and Culture, located in Punta Gorda, Florida. For over thirty years, Dr. Bireda has consulted, lectured, written about, and provided assistance to school districts, law enforcement agencies, and corporations concerning issues related to race, gender, class, culture, and power. Dr. Bireda has written books related to racial disparity in discipline and personal empowerment as well as historical fiction. She is a contributor to wsimag.org. Dr. Bireda is a Florida Humanities Scholar, a historical reenactor, and a public speaker. Most importantly, Dr. Bireda is committed to using her skills to bring about racial healing and racial harmony in our nation.